THE

MAKING OF A CHRISTIAN COLLEGE IN INDIA

THE
MAKING OF A CHRISTIAN COLLEGE
IN INDIA

BEING A HISTORY OF
REID CHRISTIAN COLLEGE, LUCKNOW

BRENTON THOBURN BADLEY

GYAN

Published by

Gyan Publishing House
5, Ansari Road
Daryaganj, New Delhi-110002
Phone: 011-47034999, 9811692060
E-mail: books@gyanbooks.com

Distribution Network
gyanbooks.com
India, USA, Canada, UK, Australia

ISBN: 978-93-7133-002-2 (HB)

First Published, 1906

2nd Impression 2025

Printed at: Gyan Press, Delhi.

THE MAKING OF A CHRISTIAN COLLEGE IN INDIA
Arthur BRENTON THOBURN BADLEY

THE
MAKING OF A CHRISTIAN COLLEGE IN INDIA.

Non nobis solum sed
toti mundo nati.

The Main Building of Reid Christian College, Lucknow.

THE MAKING OF A CHRISTIAN COLLEGE IN INDIA:

BEING A HISTORY OF

REID CHRISTIAN COLLEGE, LUCKNOW.

BY THE

REV. BRENTON THOBURN BADLEY, M.A.,

Professor of English and Philosophy in

REID CHRISTIAN COLLEGE.

1906.

PREFACE.

The story of the founding of Reid Christian College which appears in these pages, is the outcome of an effort of the writer to fulfill the duties of the College Historian, to which office he was last year elected by the Alumni Association of the College. In this account of the College is embodied the result of three year's research. In the effort to include everything of importance, no source of information was knowingly overlooked. Nearly every veteran concerned with those early days was laid under tribute for information, while a very large correspondence covering the past twenty-five years was read with great care and utilized wherever it seemed advisable. If, however, events of importance and interest should have escaped the writer, he will consider it a favour if those who can vouch for them will communicate with him concerning them.

The Jubilee year of Indian Methodism seems a most fitting time for looking backward to those interesting days of beginnings

It is hoped that the history of such a representative institution, casting so much incidental light upon characters of importance in the early history of our Church in India, will not be without some interest.

The first part of this story, including chapters I to X, appeared originally in the columns of "THE INDIAN WITNESS," and for the reproduction of it here the author is indebted to the Editor of that paper. The remaining chapters have been written under the disadvantages consequent on writing of events of recent years. It is hoped that sometime in the future some one may prepare a revised and enlarged edition.

The writer's thanks are due to all who have helped him in the preparation of this little book, including Rev. J. H. Messmore, Rev. Henry Mansell, Rev. T. S. Johnson and particularly Rev. J. W. Waugh, who furnished much valuable material on the history of the early days.

B. T. B.

"DILARAM", LUCKNOW,
December 15, 1906.

CONTENTS.

APPENDIX.

List of Illustrations.

Making a Christian College

CHAPTER I.

Early Visions.

WHEN THE METHODIST EPISCOPAL CHURCH entered India as a Missionary Society, it was only to be expected that among the agencies employed by it to spread the news of the Gospel would be the educational one. The history of the Church in the past has shown that her policy was ever to count Christian educational institutions among the strongholds of the Christian faith. It thus transpired that even before the end of the first century of her history in America, she had built up fourteen Colleges and over seventy academies. With such a record in America, it could e sily have been seen at the outset that our Church in India was sure to enlist the school and College in carrying out the great work for which the Master had commissioned American Methodism.

Perhaps the earliest reference to the part that the Methodist Episcopal Church in

India was to have in the sphere of education, is to be found in a printed statement sent out from Lucknow on March 21st, 1859. The paper is entitled "Statement and Appeal," being an effort to raise Rs. 60,000 in India for the purpose of building twenty residences for as many new missionaries who were shortly expected to re-inforce the three who then represented our Church in this land. The appeal is signed by "W. Butler, D. D., R. Pierce, A. M., and J. L. Humphrey." Referring to the policy of the Mission, the following statement is made:—

"We now occupy Lucknow, Moradabad and Naini Tal. And, as fast as our brethren arrive we contemplate opening our mission in Sitapore, Shahjahanpore, Bareilly, Badaun, Pilibhit and Bijnour, occupying each station strongly, and reaching the smaller places around them by a regular system of itinerancy and the establishment of schools."

It is noteworthy that not only were all these stations duly occupied, but the system of schools was projected which has made our Church one of he greatest educational forces in this land.

The Rev. WILLIAM BUTLER, D.D.,
Founder of the Methodist Episcopal Mission in India.
Born 1818, Died 1899.

Early Visions.

The value of the school as an evangelistic agency was never under-estimated by our Church in India. Five years later, when the "India Mission Conference" was organized, the statistics showed that there were schools in every centre. Lucknow early became a centre of educational activity. As early as 1862 a central school-house was in process of erection in Hosainabad, the part of the city first chosen as a site for the Mission. The pioneer in the actual educational work in Lucknow was the Rev. J. H. Messmore, who arrived in India in 1861, hailing from Canada *via* the United States. From 1861 to 1871 he gave himself to building up the schools of our Mission in Lucknow, and may, in a special sense, be said to have laid the foundation of our educational work in India. His special aptitude for such work may well be realized when we find him, for forty-five years after his arrival in the country, still in educational work, building up a High School in the mountain station of Pauri.

The words of Bishop Thomson in his opening address at the organization of the

India Mission Conference in 1864 may well be reproduced here to show what ground he considered our Church should occupy in regard to this vital educational question. As we read his glowing words let us be thankful that at the laying of the foundation-stone of our work in this land there were present those master-builders, who looked far into the future and built for an allround, thoroughly developed work. In speaking of the surest and safest avenue of approach to the Hindu and Mohammedan mind, Bishop Thomson said:

"We must teach the Natural Sciences, and show how the universe is governed by fixed laws devised by an infinite and eternal mind, who, nevertheless, answers prayer according to his promise, not perhaps by altering physical laws, but by adjustments of humanity to them through the higher laws of the spiritual world. Thus men will dread only sin, and seek relief only in prayer to our Heavenly Father through Jesus Christ his Son. We must teach the young both because of the ease with which impressions are made upon their minds and because of the durability of such impressions, which are woven with the very texture of the soul. If you would write your words in a book, if you would cut them in the lead with a stilet of iron, if you would drive them with chisel and mallet into the rock, if you would send them down the ages and centuries and millenniums, aye, into eternity, write upon the young soul. In estimating your work men may count your 164 converts ; look rather to your 1,322 school boys ; a few years will reduce the former to zero, but will multiply the latter by five."

The annual session of the India Mission Conference held in 1866 marks an educational epoch in our work. The following extract from the Lucknow station Report for 1865 will show what progress the schools in Lucknow had made. "The mission has seven schools in operation in the city, six were opened during 1865." Of the Hosainabad boys' school the following report is given :

"The school-house commenced in 1862 is now so far completed that all its apartments are available for use. In August the grant-in-aid was increased from Rs. 100 to Rs. 175. The total enrolment is 410. The course of study differs but little from that prescribed for the Government schools, with the addition of a daily scripture lesson."

Thus was put on foot the educational movement which to-day is the very backbone of our mission work throughout the vast extent of the great Indian Empire.

Making a Christian College.

"Previous to 1858, with the exception of a few indigenous schools hardly worth the name, there were no educational institutions in Lucknow. The King, wasting thousands of rupees in cock-fighting and on dancing-women, founded not a single school. Hence the missionaries here as elsewhere were the pioneers in educational work."

The Annual Conference of 1866, coming 100 years after the founding of American Methodism, is historically interesting, but for Indian Methodism its chief importance lies in the fact that it was at this Conference that the project of a Methodist College for India first took shape. Turning again to those old Conference records we find in the educational report the following:—

"Resolved, that we recognize it as our duty to provide opportunity for the scholars of our schools to complete their education under our direction and that when necessary, efforts be made to establish within our mission a collegiate institution to be affiliated with the Presidency University.

"Resolved, that a Committee of three be appointed to consider the matter of the establishment of such an institution and also to prepare a course of study for our schools—said Committee to report at the next session of this Conference."

Early Visions.

The Committee thus appointed consisted of the following members: H. Mansell, J. H. Messmore, and D. W. Thomas. At the same Conference a Centenary Committee, which had been previously appointed, made the following significant report :—

" Resolved, that we recognize the urgent want of a College of a high grade in connection with our work, and that we regard Lucknow as the proper location for such an institution. Resolved, that as a Conference we will attempt to raise during the coming year an endowment fund for the Lucknow school of not less than Rs. 10,000 as a nucleus around which other resources may gather sufficient to justify us in applying for an affiliation with the Calcutta University.

J. M. Thoburn
J. T. Gracey } Committee."
P. T. Wilson

This report was unanimously adopted. The reference in it to Lucknow as the proper location for the proposed College, was due to the fact that there had been some discussion as to the most suitable place. Some supported Bareilly and some Naini Tal, but Lucknow was finally chosen by a very clear majority. The wisdom of the choice has become more apparent as the years have gone by. Educationally, politically, and socially Lucknow is the first city of the Province; while as to population, it is one of the chief inland cities of India. Its location, moreover, is such as to make it of ready access from any part of Northern India—the territory from which the College most naturally draws its student—body. The Isabella Thoburn College likewise found a home in the same city, and Lucknow is to-day, from an educational point of view, the chief centre of American Methodism in India.

The report which the Centenary Committee brought in is of such interest and importance as to justify its being embodied in full. It reads as follows:—

"The Committee appointed to consider over the College enterprise in connection with our centenary subscriptions beg leave to present the following resolutions:—

'Resolved 1st, that our Centenary College be located in the city of Lucknow. 2nd, that a board of five trustees be appointed to take charge of centenary subscriptions and hold in trust all endowment funds and other property accruing to the College; said board to be appointed in the following manner and be governed by the following rules:—

1st. The Board shall consist of the Presiding Elder of the Lucknow District, the Principal of the Institution and of three additional members of Conference elected by ballot.

2nd. The Trustees shall nominate the Principal of the Institution, subject to confirmation by the appointing power of the Conference.

3rd. Trustees elected shall hold office for three years, but the first election shall be for terms of one, two and three years, so that one member may retire annually.

4th. The Principal shall nominate and the Board appoint all teachers and determine the salaries of the same.

5th. The Board shall approve the course of study and general rules of the institution.

6th. The Board shall authorize all applications for Grants-in-aid and sanction all expenditure of local funds for the College.

7th. They shall consider the general interest of the College as being specially entrusted to their care and shall devise such measures as circumstances may suggest for enlarging its endowment and increasing its efficiency.

8th. They shall invest the endowment in such a way as may promise the largest returns.'"

The following extract concerning the enterprise from the "Missionary Advocate," the official organ of our Missionary Society, which later on was supplanted by the "Gospel in All Lands," makes interesting reading after forty years:

"The Committee on the centenary celebration recommended a religious celebration to be held in each district in the latter part of October, that the object of our contribution shall be to secure a College in Lucknow, and that an effort be made to raise $5,000 towards endowment of the same, and that the presiding elders be a committee to carry out the scheme. In the discussion it was stated that there were ten thousand boys within two miles of the Mission school in Lucknow who ought to be in school; that while there were five thousand boys in the schools in Calcutta there were only one thousand in the schools of Lucknow. Yet that in Lucknow the number is growing rapidly, and three years ago there were only three or four hundred scholars in the schools of Lucknow; but the number is doubling nearly every year. These and like facts showed Lucknow clearly to be the place for it if a college enterprise was to be undertaken. The project itself was approved, among other reasons, because of the great benefit that will accrue to all our schools if they can be affiliated with a college, and the education of the students completed under our superintendence.

Thus the India mission having resolved, as was stated by one of the speakers, to take part in the celebration, it will be the first Conference in the connection to greet the sun as it rises on the morning of the Centenary Sabbath of Methodism."

With the adoption of this report by the conference of 1867, the college project was definitely launched. It is to the credit of that small body of missionaries that so soon after the occupation of this foreign field by the Missionary Society of our Church, they had the faith, wisdom and foresight to lay plans for such an institution. It was clear that they were ambassadors of the Great King who, whether in a Christian or a heathen land, were not to be satisfied with anything short of the greatest and best. They were young men who had visions, not of a Missionary Society working in a prescribed field with elementary institutions, but of a Christian Empire in the Orient, possessed of the most thoroughly equipped Christian agencies and institutions. This is just what was to be expected of such leaders as William Butler, J. M. Thoburn and E. W. Parker, and those others the record of whose lives if not so carefully preserved here below, is faithfully written in the annals of the King of Glory. Let us be thankful that there were in those early days men who, from the vantage-ground of faith, could look far into the future and see both the greatness of the work to be done, and the means necessary to its accomplishment. But many years were required for the fulfilment of those early visions. Just ten years after the appointment of the first Board of Trustees the "Centennial" school was established as the first step towards the realization of the visions of 1867. But a school was not a College, and eleven years more elapsed before the College was opened. The story of this interval of twenty-one years will require several chapters for its telling.

CHAPTER II.

Struggling for an Endowment.

If the College was not established till more than twenty years after the project had been inaugurated, it was not due to inadequate efforts to get an endowment. The measures taken to secure friends and money for the proposed institution were immediate, but only fairly successful.

At the Annual Conference of 1868, the Secretary of the College Board of Trustees, Rev. J. H. Messmore, stated that Rs. 10,000 had been subscribed. We learn from the records that of this amount Rs. 800 were given by seven missionaries, and Rs. 3,000 by General (then Major) J. Y. Gowan. This amount given by General Gowan was the beginning of the college endowment. It had been made over by him to Rev. J. H. Messmore for the school at Hosainabad, but was, on the advent of the college idea, allowed by Mr. Messmore to go towards building up an endowment for the proposed College. The missionaries' subscriptions came next in point of time;

then the various subscriptions in stations occupied by our Mission. It must be said in passing, however, that some opposition was experienced in those early efforts, which arose in our own misssonary circle. One who was present at the time, says, " Some of the missionaries were not very warm or earnest in their support of the institution, feeling that some station further north would better have been chosen". It only goes to show that all good men are not equally endowed with good judgment.

The Church at home did not respond either very readily or very liberally. Hopefulness, however, on the part of the missionaries was not lacking. The report of the Secretary of the College Board of Trustees, from which a quotation appears in the above paragraph, continues the theme thus :

" The Trustees are in correspondence with laymen in America, who will, in all probability, complete the proposed endowment of Rs. 25,000 by the close of the year. But twenty-five thousand rupees are a very small portion of endowment necessary, and the Trustees are profoundly impressed with the necessity of speedily raising the endowment to at least Rs. 100,000, and in their opinion the employment of a special agent in America is the most feasible way of accomplishing this purpose. In conclusion, the Trustees would re-iterate their profound conviction of the necessity of the proposed College ; also their assurance that with the blessing of God on our united efforts the work will reach a successful completion ; and now call upon the conference to unite with them in the determination that they will strive to place our College on a prosperous basis."

Subsequent events showed, however, that the Church at home was not yet ready to see such an enterprise through the eyes of those who were planning for it on the field. Even twenty years later it was with great difficulty that a man was found at home who would invest even the modest sum of $15,000 in the College when it was already on its feet.

In 1867 the Board of Trustees prepared a special circular for the Church at home, entitled "The Mission College in India." This appeal states the whole educational problem so clearly and forcibly that a quotation from its more interesting parts will, doubtless, be a valuable addition to this history of our college enterprise in India. It will also shed most interesting light upon the educational field which lay before the Mission when work was first undertaken. It says :—

"Feeling well assured that the Church at home feels a deep interest in all that concerns our mission in India, and that all information tending to show our progress or the character of our work is eagerly sought after whenever published, we have thought it simply our duty to send home a brief sketch of the origin, present condition, and prospects, of the college enterprise which our young Conference has undertaken. This is the most important enterprise in which we have yet embarked, and the future prosperity of our work is bound up in it to an extent which few persons outside of India can well appreciate.

"At the commencement of our work in India, small schools were established in connection with the different stations, and an attempt made, as is usual in foreign missions, to inculcate religious truth through the medium of Christian books and teachers. A few years' experience, however, fully convinced our brethren that our schools must hold a very different position from that at first contemplated, and that we must not aim merely at gaining access to a few children, but must, to a great extent, fight our battle on the educational field.

Struggling for an Endowment.

In Africa, the South Seas, and other semi-barbarous countries, and even in China, the case is different, but here we find ourselves in the midst of a great educational movement. The intellect of India is awaking from its sleep of more than twenty centuries and everywhere the youth may be seen thronging towards the school-room. We had boldly entered the country and challenged Mohammedanism and Hinduism to combat, and now we had no alternative, short of retreat, left us, save that of manfully trying to meet the momentous responsibilities which this intellectual awakening had imposed upon us. It is idle to talk of confining our work to preaching alone. As well try to persuade the Church at home to abolish her Colleges and Seminaries. We had no choice. To have shrunk from our responsibilities, would have been to postpone our final triumph for generations to come and consign the intellect of the country to a depraved infidelity, compounded of the superstition of the Hindu, the bigotry of the Mohammedan, and the Sadducean heartlessness of the European rationalist. We saw clearly that Christianity must at once assume her full responsibility in trying to guide this educational movement, so as to make it a blessing instead of a curse to India, and hence were obliged to adapt our plans to the emergency; giving our schools a higher grade and wider field in which to operate, than is usual in missions in other countries.

"This policy became the more imperatively necessary from the fact that non-Christian schools, supported by Government, were organized in all important towns and cities, and that these schools, although professedly 'neutral' in religious matters, were everywhere recognized by Hindus and Mohammedans as peculiarly theirs. In this case, as in the Border States at the commencement of the war, neutrality practically means an interdict of total silence on one party, and a wide latitude to all others. We had to compete with these schools, and although our resources were seldom more than half of theirs, we were able in most cases, with God's help, to do so successfully. Meanwhile our Mission field was extended, new stations occupied, new schools organized and thus every year our educational interests became more important. The result was that when we met in Conference in February, 1866, about eight years after the organization of our first little school by Dr. Butler and his associates at Naini Tal, it was found that we had no less than 2,005 pupils enrolled in our different schools.

"Meanwhile a new difficulty has been encountered in our more advanced schools. A great many colleges have sprung up throughout the country, in affiliation with the Calcutta University, and institutions chartered by the Government with full University powers; and our more advanced students began to leave us in order to secure the superior advantages which these institutions were able to offer. We began to discover too that there was very great danger of our schools losing the confidence of the public, chiefly owing to this cause. It was plain that they must sink to the rank of inferior schools unless kept fully abreast with their competitors. It was seen by all that a College was a necessity. A central institution, more or less directly connected with all our schools, seemed necessary to keep our students from leaving us, and save the educational prestige of the Mission.

"We are well aware that we have undertaken a most gigantic task. We have most formidable competition to contend with, we are strangers in a strange land. We do not profess to know where even this small endowment is to be secured; and when it is all gathered in we know that our work will be but begun. Yet we do not hesitate to express our full confidence in the final success of the enterprise. We believe that in a country where the utmost care is taken to divorce education and religion, God will not fail to honour and bless the College that writes CHRISTIAN over its portals. Meanwhile we commend our infant College to the sympathy and prayers of those who feel an interest in our work, and we cannot close without expressing a hope that among them God will raise up some who will yet prove friends indeed to the first Methodist College in Asia."

J. W. Waugh, Chairman. J. H. Messmore, Secretary. D. W. Thomas, Treasurer. J. M. Thoburn, Agent. T. S. Johnson, M. D.	Board of Trustees.

The mission field itself was not neglected in the efforts to arouse the Church in America. During the winter of 1867-8 an opportunity for reaching the wealthy and those in high social and political positions was afforded the friends of the embryo College which was improved to the best of their ability. The historian, being indebted to the Rev. J. W. Waugh, D. D. for this interesting bit of history, cannot do better than to quote his version of the incident.

"During the cold season of 1867-8 Sir John Lawrence, Viceroy and Governor-General, was to hold a Durbar in Lucknow, and the M. E. missionaries were all on the *qui vive* to meet the many visitors from all parts of the country and enlist their interest in the proposed Mission or Christian College, even though one of the functions of the Governor-General while in Lucknow was to lay the foundation stone of the great Taluqdars' institution, Canning College. A meeting was planned to be held in the Hindustani Church on new Cantonment Road, and many invitations were sent to those who we hoped might be or become interested in our college project. A fair attendance, mostly missionaries, listened to the eloquent speeches, though every day of Durbar week and every evening was crowded with brilliant events at Government House and elsewhere. The missionaries called upon a wealthy gentleman, a merchant from Calcutta, to kindly take the chair and preside; this he was greatly pleased to do! He spoke very strongly and favourably of the College enterprise, got off more than an ordinary share of the stock platitudes concerning education, and informed his audience that it was education that forms the common mind, and that also as the twig is bent the tree in inclined! (Applause.) But *the* applause came later when the speaker said that not only had presiding at this meeting given him great pleasure, but that he wished to increase and continue that pleasure by giving a *donation*, as Americans call it, or a gift, a subscription, to so worthy an object. (Hand-clapping and Hear! Hear! on the part of the missionaries, and a few English-speaking native gentlemen.) The meeting closed, and those most interested in the college enterprise were very hopeful, voted the meeting a success, and had visions as they talked together in the Church; and, after their tired heads sought rest on their primitive *charpais*, visions of a *donation* that would make a fine college building, a staff of learned professors in well-endowed chairs, in short, a fully equipped Christian college ready for the highest education and evangelization of North India, a glorious certainty.

"In the afternoon of the next day a red-coated *chaprasi* came to the Mission house and deposited in the hand of the missionary a note, not a currency note for Rs. 10,000, but a written chit saying that the chairman of last evening's interesting meeting had pleasure in sending in as his contribution the sum of twenty sicca rupees, *which please accept*, etc. The presiding elder accepted the rupees, credited the amount to the College fund, and did not kill the *chaprasi*, as would, to the unregenerate heart, have seemed appropriate. And he did not call a meeting of his fellow missionaries, to break to them the good news—in fact the matter was barred as a subject for reference in subsequent social or religious conversation."

Such were the early disappointments encountered by these struggling heroes. It brings the smile to our lips as we look back forty years, but it brings also the glow of appreciation to the heart, and the realization that the success of the present rests upon just such energy, resourcefulness and true ambition. But we accord these men a larger share of credit when we see how they followed up this unsuccessful attempt. Here, again, the writer is indebted to Dr. Waugh, and will, with much pleasure, once more call into requisition his ready pen. He continues the narrative as follows:

"But our determination remained firm that we must not only raise funds for the College, but that we must secure recognition from the local and general Government. Lord Lawrence was known and recognized as the friend of education and of missionary effort and enterprise in this direction. He must be appealed to. As every hour of his stay in Lucknow was fully occupied, the only chance seemed to be for a small deputation to wait on him and ascertain when he could give us a half hour's interview. Accompanied by Bro. H. Jackson I hastened to Government House, where the Governor-General was staying. Sir John Strachey, as Chief Secretary of Oudh, being host. On sending in our cards, we were met at the inner entrance by Sir Henry Norman, at that time Secretary to the Viceroy. He intimated that it might be difficult to have an interview now, as the Viceroy was just dressing to go out and meet an important engagement with some taluqdars, some of Oudh's nobility. Lord Lawrence apparently overhearing what was said, called out to his Secretary, 'Sir Henry! If those missionary gentlemen will consent to come into my room while I am washing my face, and combing my hair, I shall be delighted to see them and talk to them, for it is my only chance!' We went in all smiling at the free and easy reception ; and it did not take long to place our college enterprise before him, and express our hope that Government would recognize us and our efforts in some substantial way. He was very free to respond and say he was in entire sympathy with our scheme; and that when the application came before him in an official way he would do all in his power to help us. He wished us success, and said the official application should come up to him through the Local Government—(this we knew, but hoped in some way to get over as easily as possible, as Sir John Strachey was not a friend of missions or mission enterprises). Lord Lawrence closed by saying, as we arose to leave, 'I am glad you came, though I could only receive you in so very informal a way, and give you so little time ; but this I wish to say, what I do and can do as Governor-General is one thing and what I do, as John Lawrence is quite another thing !' This was hopeful and pleased us very much."

This certainly *was* hopeful ; but, so far as history has anything to say, it made little difference whether it was officially or privately that Lord Lawrence was interested in the College. Yet the cause of missions had a staunch advocate in Lord Lawrence : not

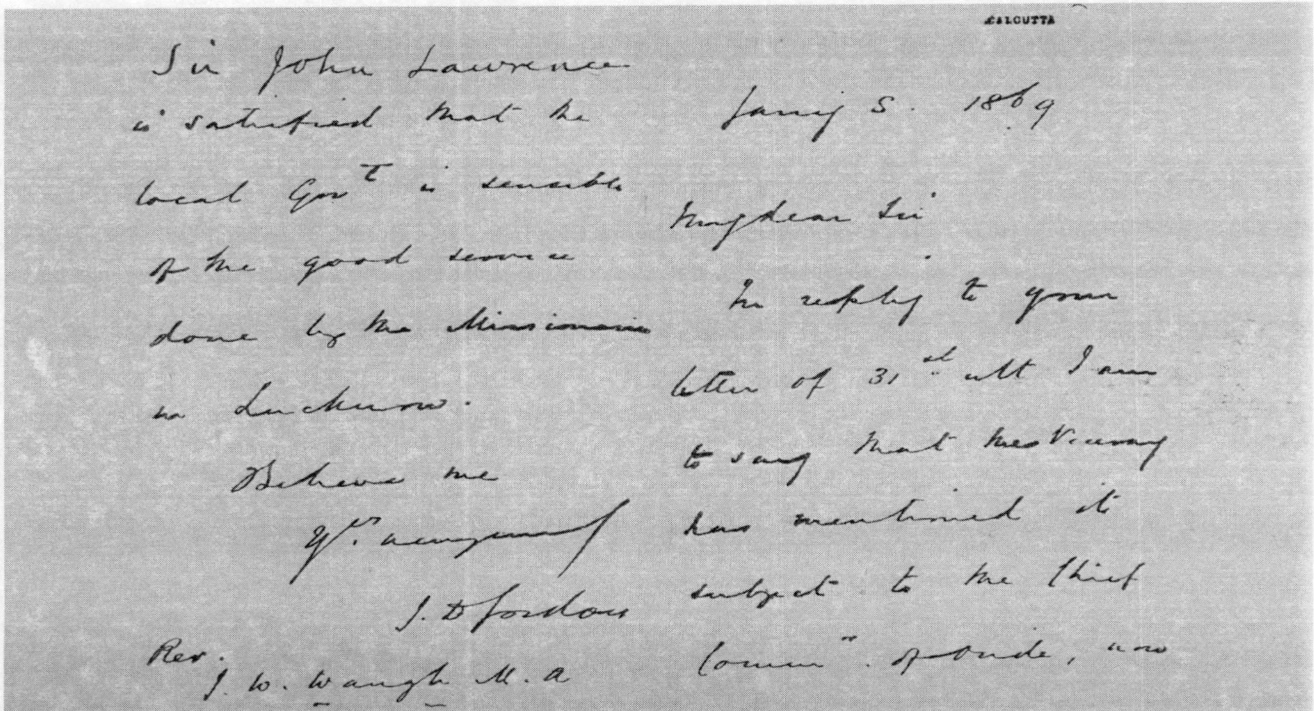

CALCUTTA

Jany 5. 1869

My dear Sir

In reply to your letter of 31st ult I am to say that the Viceroy has mentioned the subject to the Chief Commr. of Oude, and

Sir John Lawrence is satisfied that the local Govt is sensible of the good service done by the Missionaries in Lucknow.

Believe me
Yrs. very truly
J. D. Gordon

Rev. J. W. Waugh M.A

Facsimile of the Viceregal Letter
Showing Pages 1 and 4.

many years before this event he it was who said: "If England had not been afraid of professing her Christian principles in India, the Mutiny, which cost her £200,000,000 sterling and rivers of blood would never have occurred; notwithstanding all that English people have done to benefit India, the missionaries have done more than all other agencies combined."

This promising event was followed up by a special letter to the Secretary of Government, sent at a time when the Commissioner of Oudh was on a visit to Calcutta. The letter requested that the Governor-General would be good enough to see the Chief Commissioner of Oudh and urge that some action be taken favouring the Mission College project. In reply a letter came from the Secretary which reads as follows:—

"GOVERNMENT HOUSE, Calcutta, Jan. 8, 1869.

My Dear Sir: In reply to your letter of the 31st ultimo, I am to say that the Viceroy has mentioned the subject to the Chief Commissioner of Oudh now in Calcutta. His Excellency does not doubt that when the question of Grant-in-aid comes before him officially Mr. Davis will do all that he properly can to meet the wishes of the Revd. missionaries. It is absolutely necessary that discussion by the educational authorities should precede a decision on so important a matter. Sir John Lawrence is satisfied that the Local Government is sensible of the good service done by the missionaries in Lucknow.

Yours very truly,
J. D. GORDON."

The hint given in the letter from the Viceroy as to the part which the Provincial Government must play in the matter, was not lost on those who had the college enterprise on their hearts. But the local Government was very slow to do anything in the interest of the College. Records do not show that anything was received as a direct result from those efforts. It was not till twenty years later that the College was to receive any financial aid from the Government.

CHAPTER III.

Resting on the Oars.

The period of strenuous activity in behalf of the College was followed by one of comparative rest. This was due in large part to the paucity of men, the urgent needs of the evangelistic work drawing every available man into that form of work. The endowment grew but its growth was slow. After two years the College undertaking being very little nearer completion than in 1868, the missionaries again felt the pressing need of such an institution. In 1870 the Conference Committee on education made the following statement in their report :—

"When our first schools were opened, little more than ten years ago, none supposed we would so soon be involved in a gigantic educational work, such as is reported to this Conference. No less than 115 schools are now under the care of this mission, with 4,524 boys and girls enrolled, while a boundless field invites us on every side."

After noting this rapidly enlarging work, and referring to the increased demand for a

College, the Committee on education continues its report as follows :—

"Such an institution vigorously conducted would be valuable to us as a mission, and we should keep it steadily in view in all our plans."

The Board of Trustees for the proposed College was constituted an Educational Board. This was done in the interest of higher education, and the duties of the Board were defined as the supervision of the educational work of the entire mission, with special attention to be given to the schools of the highest grade. In the following year this Board, in its annual report to the Conference, said:

"As we have every reason to believe that in a very few years a large number of Christian youth will be dependent upon us for their education, we should never cease our efforts to furnish them every opportunity of completing their education under our own special direction, and we are therefore more and more impressed with the necessity for the establishment of a mission college in our midst."

In 1872 a large part of the endowment was invested in two bungalows in the Lucknow

Cantonment, Rs. 5,000 being invested in one and Rs. 1,800 in the other,—"leaving Rs. 1,000 still uninvested." The same report makes the encouraging statement that a subscription of Rs. 6,000 had been added to the endowment.

At the Conference held in 1874 the endowment fund stood as follows: Invested in bungalows Rs. 9,300; subscription received in New York (not then realized in India) Rs. 2,000; Unproductive land in the United States, (Rs. 3,000 or) Rs. 4,000 making a total of Rs. 15,300. A hopeful feature of the report was the statement, "this endowment has been enlarged from its own income by nearly Rs. 2,000 during the year." In 1875 the endowment was reported as amounting to Rs. 17,753. Thus it is seen that eight years after the enterprise had been formally undertaken, the modest sum of Rs. 25,000, which had originally been aimed at as an endowment, had not yet been secured.

This term of enforced delay is a matter of general regret to us as we look back on that period. The money was the chief need—or to put it in another way, the men were needed who could bend their energies to the securing of the necessary funds. In 1885 when the Rev. B. H. Badley was making an appeal for the College, he wrote of this period as follows :

> "It is to be regretted that the school was not at once opened ; this was impossible owing to the paucity of labourers (there being but two missionaries in Lucknow in 1868 and 1869) and the urgent demands of other and older forms of work. The time was favourable and the beginning encouraging, but the missionaries, already overworked, were obliged to postpone their efforts. Much was thus lost ; promptness in entering the open door, would have given the Mission a school which, long ere this might have won for our Church in India laurels worth wearing."

The original idea had been that the large and flourishing school at Hosainabad, which had been built up by Rev. J. H. Messmore, would be the germ from which the College would develop. The plan, however, was destined to failure. The first property of the Mission in Lucknow had been purchased in Hosainabad. This property, now at the extreme west end of the city and forming a portion of the fine gardens surrounding the clock tower, had at that time a fairly central location. The most thickly populated portion of the city lay near at hand, being of ready access for evangelistic work and affording a fine field for educational purposes. But the trend of population was eastward, and by 1870 our missionaries realized that though for the present the site occupied would be central enough for all mission purposes, the day was not distant when the Hosainabad site would be left on the western edge of the great city. The old Mohammedan city was around them, but the new city due to English enterprise and the location of a large British garrison, was making a centre, some three miles eastward.

It is not so difficult to see what should be done as it is to do it. When a site had been taken up, mission houses had been built or purchased, a little cemetery had forced itself upon the mission where slept J. R. Downey, the first missionary of the Methodist Episcopal Church to fall in India, and especially when a large and prosperous school in a fine building of its own spoke eloquently for the old place, it was a very difficult matter to turn the back upon the site first chosen and now endeared by many precious memories. But Providence was willing to lend a hand at this juncture, and make it easy to do what the interests of the mission required. In 1870 the modest little Goomtee, swelling with pride on account of large gifts from above, overflowed its banks and paid an unwelcome visit to the mission premises. Its call was so prolonged that the foundations of the large school house were washed out and the building—the pride of the mission—collapsed. Such was the untimely end of the school which it was intended should develop into the College. The question of changing the mission centre to suit the shifting population was now rendered easy. Rev. J. M. Thoburn and Rev, J. H. Messmore being then in charge of the work, began to cast about for a new location, and in 1871 they purchased the property known as " Inayat Bagh" some two miles east and south of the

Hosainabad site. This was destined to become the cradle of the College.

When the distruction of the Hosainabad school and the subsequent abandonment of the old site have been taken into consideration, as partly accounting for the delay in establishing the College seen in the visions of 1866, it still remains an open question why the years from 1871-77 were allowed to go by without the initial step being taken. The Hosainabad school was transferred to Nakhas, south-east of the old site, where it continues to flourish to the present day. The transfer could not carry the school as far as "Inayat Bagh," which was a centre too far removed for Hosainabad scholars; and so far as the embryo College was concerned, the enterprise—except for experience gained—had to be begun *de novo.*

CHAPTER IV.

The Centennial School.

It was some years before the Mission was ready to open a Boarding School for Christian boys. The city schools for boys were continued, but the establishment of a school which should give promise of leading on to the long-talked of College, was yet to come. At length the demand for such an institution became so general that the school was opened, February 1, 1877, with Rev. H. Mansell as principal. The "Inayat Bagh" property itself afforded no suitable site for the school, but no funds being available for building purposes, the school was opened in a small house on the mission premises, which had formerly been used as the bindery-room of the Mission Press. This building, a part of the original line of out houses is still standing, and as the cradle of both the Ried Christian College and the Methodist Publishing House in Lucknow, it is probably as historic a building as our Mission can boast of in India. Unfortunately, in its latter years it has

The Cradle of the College, occupied during 1877.

been put to the base purposes of a cook-house and store-room.

At the Conference of 1878, Rev. H. Mansell, reporting on the work of the year, said

"The Centennial School, so called because the funds for its small endowment were (first) collected in the Centennial year of American Methodism, is a Day and Boarding school for Christian boys. Fees Rs 5 per mensem are charged for board and tuition. Twenty-six boys attended during the year. (Total enrollment 40.) The standard will be raised to Entrance to Calcutta University."

This brief report is all that is on record of the first year. Only last year, however, the historian wrote to Dr. Henry Mansell and obtained from him the following additional facts concerning those early days. It is a great pleasure to be able to quote from them.

"I lived that year in the old 'Inayat Bagh' *kothi* which was a range of old, tumble-down buildings with any number of old servants' houses and godowns which we utilized for the school, using the godowns and servants' houses for the servants and boarders, and also for one master who managed the Boarding department as well as part of the teaching. There was an old office close to the *kothi*, rather permanent and respectable which we used as the school-house, putting in a table, a desk or two and a few benches. Mr. Cunningham had tried two years before to start the school in Ghasiyari Mandi, but had given it up and had left only two or three *degchis* and *thalis* and a few *lotas* which came in use to begin with in the boarding department. We started with about five or six boys ; but the numbers increased till we closed the term with 40 boys on the roll. There were three or four large boys somewhat advanced in mathematics, and who had gone through the fourth book in English, English-grammar, and History, also two English (Eurasian) boys whom I taught in the subjects above mentioned. The oldest of the Hindustani boys (I forget his name) helped me some in teaching, and I believe went through the entire course and afterwards took his B. A. The others also did well. One of the European boys was Rabbit, a grandson of Sergeant Orman. The other European was young Hollinberry a son of a Barrister in Lucknow. He got on well and became a vakil (lawyer) and was some time practising in the courts of Lucknow. The little boys all did very well. About half of them were day pupils living in Ghasiyari Mandi. I very much enjoyed morning prayer with the boys, when the Bible was read and I explained a portion of it every morning. I usually asked the larger boys in rotation to read the Scripture lessons. At the end of the year I was appointed to Gonda and Baharaich, and the loved, learned and accomplished Dr. Badley took up the school and it grew into the present Reid Christian College."

The Centennial School was supported on the income received from the endowment of the College which had been planned for. During the infancy of the school this probably sufficed; but as early as 1881 the Principal reported that the annual income was "sufficient for the present to meet about half the current expenses of the institution."

The first advertisement of the school, in speaking of the course of study, makes the following statement :—

"We take boys of all ages and stages of progress, and advance them as fast as possible. . . Thorough, but not sectarian, instruction is given in the Bible, and strict morality is enjoined. The rudiments of vocal music are also taught."

The teachers, in addition to the Principal, included a Headmaster, a pupil tutor, a teacher for Persian and Urdu and one for Hindi and Sanskrit. Such was the humble beginning of the school which was destined to grow into Reid Christian College.

There were those who questioned the need

of such an institution. In remarking on this the writer cannot do better than to quote from one of the early reports of the school prepared by the Rev. B. H. Badley, then Principal.

"The need," he says "is apparent from the fact that the large and gradually increasing native Christian community in Oudh and the North-west Provinces has no such School. There are Orphanages to which, in too many cases, the children of poor Christians find their way, remaining for years a burden to the Mission; there are several flourishing boarding schools for girls but there is no boarding school for boys. Several mission schools have boarding departments, but these are all on a most limited scale, and there is urgent need of a school like this. If it be urged that the children of these Native Christians are just as well off in the various Government schools, it may be answered that their parents (certainly the most interested parties) do not think so, but look with hearty approval upon a Christian boarding school where their sons may obtain a first class education and at the same time be surrounded by Christian influences."

CHAPTER V.

The Coming of the Man.

In the Annual Conference appointments for 1878 the following entry may be found: "Lucknow, B. H. Badley, Principal of Centennial School" When the President of that Conference had read out this appointment, he had linked that name with the school which for the next thirteen years was to be most intimately associated with it, and which for all time was to be inseparable from it. The man with the executive ability to fulfill the visions of 1866 had appeared. The man had come on the stage of our educational action, who, under the Providence of God, was first to raise the little school into a High School giving it a new home, and then to establish the College, laying down his life only after the walls of a magnificent building were started up.

The first concern of the new Principal was to move the school into such quarters as would insure a normal and healthy growth. A log cabin may be a sufficiently good place for a President to be born in, but he must quit the log house before he can get into the "White House." The anxiety to secure a suitable building may be seen from the following lines from the pen of the Principal:

"Early in 1878, after occupying several unsuitable houses, a building was purchased, at a cost of Rs. 4,200. It had been used as a private residence, and was not well adapted to school purposes, but was the most desirable property that could be obtained. * * * The school is located between Qaisarbagh and Aminabad, opposite the Raushan-Ud-Daula *kothi*."

Some years later, in referring to those early days, Dr. Badley said:—

"From the beginning the institution had to contend against the very serious difficulty of small, unsuitable buildings. The premises have not been inviting, and the school has consequenly suffered. On one occasion the wife of a missionary came several hundred miles, bringing half a dozen boys for the school, but on account of the inferior buildings she decided to take the boys elsewhere"

This condition of things was finally remedied in 1883 when the school entered its new building at Gola Ganj.

The Coming of the Man.

The school early became a potent factor in the Christian work of the city. Dr. Badley came to Lucknow from a four years' vigorous evangelistic campaign in the Gonda District, and he carried with him into the work of the school an earnest Christian spirit. During the second year of its administration, the policy of the School regarding non-Christians was changed. The following statement appears in a historical summary:

" During the first two years only Christian students were admitted, but as others desired to attend and were willing to study the Bible and conform to all the regulations of the school, they were enrolled as day-scholars, and Christians and non-Christians are now found in all the classes. The plan has worked well, and it is hoped that the daily contact with Christian teachers and students may be the means of bringing many of the others to Christ, and that the institution may thus become a powerful evangelizing agency. The Bible is a daily text-book, and in the lower classes the Church catechisms are taught. While the school is chiefly intended for Christian boys, its projectors feel that they are justified in seeking to extend the sphere of its helpful influence, and thus, following the example of the Chirstian Colleges in Calcutta, Madras, and elsewhere, they do not close its doors to the Hindu and Mohammedan youth who seek admission."

The teaching staff was gradually enlarged, and the wisdom of founding such a school was soon manifested. In a few years the institution had attracted to itself "students from all parts of Central and North India, from Calcutta, Allahabad, Cawnpore, Agra, Gujrat, Jaipore, Moradabad, Bareilly, Shahjahanpore, Pauri and elsewhere."

"The patronage of the school," continues the Principal, "is not confined to our own Church. Students in attendance have represented the Church of England, the Presbyterian, United Presbyterian, Wesleyan, Baptist and other Churches, and thus it will be in the future. Within a circle of four hundred and fifty miles there is no other boarding school for Christian boys, and in the territory thus indicated there are several flourishing missions."

This last statement goes to show that we were early in the educational field, and set an example which has been followed by every Mission in the area mentioned.

It will be unnecessary to follow in detail the activities of the school during the five

The First Permanent Home of the Centennial School.
Occupied by the School from 1878 to 1883.

years that Dr. Badley administered its affairs previous to his furlough in 1883. A summary of the results of these five years will be a sufficient indication of the progress made. There were great difficulties in those early days, but the rate at which the school grew clearly indicated that its success was assured. The total yearly attendance from the beginning was as follows:—1877, 40; 1878, 53; 1879, 110; 1880, 125; 1881, 184; 1882, 311; 1883, 400. Thus in 1883 when Dr. Badley proceeded to America on furlough, he had the joy of seeing the small attendance of the first year multiplied by ten. A still more important improvement was that the school in 1882 was advanced to the standard of a High School, matriculating its first class of five students in December of that year. This was really the second step towards the attainment of the ideal of 1866, one without which the College itself could not have come. It took five years, after the school had been opened, to make this step, and six to make the next one to the College.

The difficulty of getting a suitable site for the school and erecting for it a building which should be adequate to its needs, was one which was felt from the first. Dr. Badley's faith and spirit of hopefulness never failed him. As early as 1879 he was casting about for a permanent site. His optimism led him to expect the best things. On one occasion in the year 1879 he was walking past the present magnificent site of the High School. It was at that time little better than a jungle, covered here and there with castor bean plants, corn and tobacco fields. There was little to make it attractive, but he turned to his companion and said, "Do you see that corn field ? Right across there the High School will stand. And on the little hill where that little palm tree grows our house will stand. Over there (indicating a site behind that of the school) will be dormitories and a gymnasium." His companion discouraged the dream, saying that the land was *Nazul* and that the Government would never sell a property so near *The* "*Residency*. "You will see", said Dr. Badley, and when you live in our house upon that little knoll, I'll say I told you so !" Three years later the site had been purchased from the Government and preparations were under way for building the new High School; and three years from the latter date the Principal's new house on "Residency Hill" was ready for occupation. Thus was it ever with him whose faith in this enterprise was as sure and as great as his faith in his Divine Master. This was the man who in 1872 on the eve of sailing for India had said—"I rejoice that Christianity *is confident.* The basis of its faith is strong. It is evermore saying, as it looks away from earth and the earthly, 'In the name of the Lord our God we will set up our banners.' * * * I had rather be with a dozen working Christians, battling for God against Satan, than to have walked up and down the Field of the Cloth of Gold. God's workers wear purple every day."

The Conference of 1883 granted Dr. Badley a furlough to America as his first term of ten years had expired, but as the Indian shores faded in the distance, there rose before him the vision of a Christian College in Lucknow. With the High School an established fact, with 400 students thronging its halls, and with a new building soon to be erected on a site unsurpassed in the city for such purposes, the dreams of 1866 for a Methodist College in India were near fulfilment. In at least one man's mind the vision of the College was never absent. But the dreamer was going home on furlough to work.

CHAPTER VI.

The Centennial High School.

The Conference which granted a furlough to Dr. Badley also appointed the Rev. J. W. Waugh, D. D., to succeed him as Principal of the Centennial High School. The choice was an admirable one, and especially as the erection of the new High School building required wise superintendence. To this work Dr. Waugh immediately addressed himself. His description of the new site is interesting.

"The present site of the Centennial High School building had been secured by Dr. Badley before he left for America, and funds almost sufficient to put up the first permanent edifice on the site. This site, 'Residency Hill,' was cleared and levelled early in 1883, plans drawn, the foundations laid, and materials, brick, stone, lime, brought upon the ground. The site proved to be a most remarkable one. Up to the mutiny days the place had been thickly studded with buildings, shops, native residences, etc. The excavation for foundations had to go down very deep to get good ground: for some parts of the building we had to dig from 13 ft. to 17ft. deep, and we came upon an old *pukka* wall, two *pukka* roads crossing, and two or three wells, the latter having to be filled to the level with mud and rubble from old buildings, which we puddled with streams of water from the mission well. The old roads made splendid foundations but ran in such very devious directions as to be useless for our purposes. In a comparatively short time, with constant supervision, the foundations were in, and the day appointed for the laying of the foundation stone had come."

The laying of the foundation stone was an occasion of exceptional interest. To the older men present, it must have brought up memories of the old Hosainabad school. Especially can we imagine the thoughts which passed through the mind of Mr. Messmore, who just twenty years before had been present at the laying of the foundation stone of our first school building in Lucknow—in India. The Principal gives the following account of the ceremony:

"It was a hot afternoon, May 1, 1883. The box with the usual contents was ready. A silver trowel made for the purpose was put in the hands of the kind lady who had responded to our invitation to lay the stone, Mrs. Forbes, wife of the Commissioner of Lucknow, and with singing and prayer

The Centennial High School, Lucknow.
Built in 1883.

and all appropriate ceremonies, in the midst of a great gathering of people the stone was pronounced duly and properly laid."

The Programme of this interesting occasion is given below in full:—

CENTENNIAL HIGH SCHOOL.

LAYING FOUNDATION STONE.

TUESDAY, 1ST MAY, 1883.

Sipas Nama ... SHANKER DAYAL, FARHA

Scripture Lesson ... REV. DR. JOHNSON.

HYMN.

1. The Lord our God alone is strong;
   His hands build not for one brief day;
His wondrous works, through ages long,
   His wisdom and his power display.

2. His mountains lift their solemn forms,
   To watch in silence o'er the land;
The rolling ocean, rocked with storms,
   Sleeps in the hollow of his hand.

3. Beyond the heavens He sits alone,
   The universe obeys his nod;
The lightning-rifts disclose his throne,
   And thunders voice the name of God.

4. Thou sovereign God, receive this gift
   Thy willing servants offer thee;
Accept the prayers that thousands lift,
   And let these halls accepted be.

5. And let those learn, who here shall meet,
   True wisdom is with reverence crowned,
And Science walks with humble feet
   To seek the God that Faith hath found.

Making a Christian College.

Prayer ... ... REV. J. H. MESSMORE

Depositing Corner stone Box ... REV. J. W. WAUGH, PRINCIPAL.

Laying the Stone ... MRS. FORBES.

GIT.

Malika salàmat ho—Yá Allàh, Malika ko
Rakh tù bakhair : Kar use fathmand,
Khush-hál aur sar-buland, Ràj us ka iqbàlmand;
Malika ki khair!

Malika ki khair!

Shortly after this auspicious event, word was received from Dr. Badley that a clock and bell might soon be expected from America. These were due to the efforts of Dr. and Mrs. Badley at home, half the cost of the bell being secured by Bishop Bowman and the other half through the efforts of Mrs. Badley. It is interesting to note that of the amount raised for the tower clock Rs. 100 are credited to the sale of "Residency Bricks" which had been taken home for this purpose, and Rs. 22 to "R. C. Bose's lecture at Indianola."* Thus both the little flat Indian brick and one of India's own sons, the finished product of mission institutions,

* In the State of Iowa, U.S.A.

were helping the cause of Christian education in India. Dr. Waugh makes the following reference to the subject :—

"A clock and bell were announced as on their way out from America and a tower had to be erected without plans or specifications other than those suggested to the Principal by the exigencies of the case. But the tower was builded after the style of the old Norman builders, and though 'homely as mud' the blame must belong to the Normans! The great Hosainabad tower was about to have a clock put up—the tower and clock at a cost sixteen times that of our school building, tower clock and all—and two clockmakers were sent out to India from London to put up the clock and make it run! With me, the making and fitting of the dials was the hardest part, as nothing but the wheels, axles, pendulum, nuts and screws came, and had to be put together by a novice. At last it was done—a fact accomplished, and *Residency Hill* had the first clock and bell in all the regions of Oudh and round about.',

When completed the new building had cost about Rs. 35,000, of which amount the Government had given Rs. 15,000 as a building grant. Some time after *Zion's Herald* contained the following words from the pen of Rev. J. Mudge, a former missionary, and from 1873-82 Editor of the "Indian Witness" (then the "Lucknow Witness"):—

Lucknow must always be one of the most important cities in India, and we have done well as a Church in planting ourselves there so strongly. We have secured a grand position in that old historic capital which will be a cause of increased rejoicing as the years go on. And among the many Methodist institutions which are making their mark for Jesus upon the hundreds and thousands there, the Centennial School is by no means the least. It is plainly destined to be a mighty power in the land, training young men to work for Christ. The school has at last found a permanent and beautiful home on grounds adjoining the far-famed Lucknow "Residency." The *campus* embraces nine acres and, as an English official recently remarked, "is the finest site in Lucknow." It is admirably adapted to school purposes as it is entirely removed from other buildings and is on an elevation which renders it a most healthy location. The new building, a fine large brick edifice is 64 by 100 feet with twelve (nine) recitation rooms and a large chapel; it is surmounted by a tower 60 feet high in which are a clock and bell, the first of the kind in this part of India."

In December 1883, Dr. William Butler on a tour through India visited the school and presided at the formal opening of the new school building. His impressions as they were given to the public in the columns of *Zion's Herald* the next year make very interesting reading. Among other things, he said:

"Hardly anything that I saw in our Mission impressed me more as an instrument of great power for evangelising than did that school in the centre of that great city. I was honoured to make the address on the day of its dedication during my recent visit. When I remembered my first reception twenty-seven years before and how I had to be mounted on an elephant and guided by a sepoy with his sword drawn in his hand, as I went through those bazaars, and now in returning to find myself in that Christian School in that city, then so fierce and fanatical now so tolerant and even generous, I realised with amazement what God had wrought. The magnificent site secured, the $4,500 contributed by the native municipality and the Government towards its erection, the three hundred and fifty students, the crowded audience, among whom were many of the *elite* of Lucknow, and the Commissioner of Oudh (the governor of its 11,000,000 people) in the chair presiding—how wonderful it all seemed to me! And there was the Bible read and our hymns sung and prayer offered and a Christian education advocated without let or hindrance in *that* presence! Truly may we exclaim, 'Thou art the God that doeth wonders. Thou hast declared thy strength among the people."

At this early stage of our higher educational work we were brought to face the problem of co-education. For several months two young ladies from the Lal Bagh Girls' School studied maltrematics with our boys. The experiment, carried to the extent that it was, proved successful enough, but there was no occasion to continue it. Nearly twenty years later, when on account of Miss Thoburn's death from cholera and the danger of the disease spreading throughout the Woman's College, classes were closed, all the students for two weeks attended the classes of Reid Christian College. The later and larger experiment was also successful, but there was no necessity of continuing it. Not only has the time for co-education in this country not arrived, but there are few indeed who advocate it or would care to see it introduced.

CHAPTER VII.

Visions Again.

The progress of the Centennial High School during Dr. Badley's furlough in 1883-84 was very satisfactory. No changes were introduced by Dr. Waugh in the scholastic arrangements, and the staff continued to do good work. The numbers continued to increase, and the praise of the school was on the lips of all who visited it.

The Annual Conference which met in January 1885 reappointed Rev B. H. Badley as Principal of the school. He returned to the work full of enthusiasm in behalf of the enterprise, and set to work immediately to realise, if possible, the visions of a College which he had seen even before completing his first term of service. It was not a subject which he kept under his hat. It was not a pet scheme of his own which he had evolved after due reflection. It was the college idea which was born twenty years before in the Centennial year of American Methodism; it was a renewed vision of a

Methodist College for India, the need of which had been so often proclaimed. But the Church in India needed a man who would not only get a full view of the great institution which had been planned, but would devote his life to making those ideas live in brick and stone, Faculty and students, heart and mind. It was executive ability which was needed now, ability not only to see a thing but to make others see it also, power to raise up friends for the project, and a devotion which could and would surmount all obstacles. For such work as this Dr. Badley was admirably fitted, and the Conference, with the record of the past before it, knew what it was doing when it reappointed him to this arduous task. Probably no one dreamed that he had but six years of life before him, but he set to work with an energy which makes us think that he himself might have had an inkling of it.

As early as 1883, Dr. Badley had been in the field with an appeal for the prospective College. A pamphlet entitled "A Methodist College for India" was issued by him in America, published in New York by Phillips and Hunt. This gives a brief history of the school from its beginning, and sets forth the need of such an institution, making a strong plea and a forcible appeal for funds. This he did, not unofficially but as the authorised "Agent" for the institution while on furlough, which responsibility he had been given at the Annual Conference of 1883. Meanwhile the Church papers were kept busy setting up articles from his pen. These were considerably varied in their titles, but invariably led on to the supreme subject a Methodist College for India. Indeed, a large volume would be the result if all such appeals, tracts, and articles should be published in one cover. One wonders now why the endowment and building funds did not come in sooner. But if patience was a requisite in the effort, it was not the Principal who would be found out of stock. His quiet patience and cheerful hopefulness never failed him. Moreover some of the seed sown in those early days was not to yield a harvest until years had passed; such was the $15,000 which came from Dr. J. M. Reid, ten years later; the Rs. 18,000 and Rs. 45,000 which were received twenty years after, the first amount coming from the estate of Mrs. J. M. Reid, the second from that of Mrs. Coxe. This was a harvest the seed of which he had sowed ofttimes with tears.

On resuming the work as Principal of the school in the beginning of 1885, Dr. Badley was not long in getting a fresh plea for the College into the field. In that year the Methodist Publishing House at Lucknow issued another booklet entitled, "A Methodist College for India." This was supplemented with the usual appeals and articles in the papers, and a regular stream of private correspondence. A colleague said of him that "He worked indefatigably with tongue and pen for the endowment of the institution and gave his time, his efforts, his *life* to this work."

It will be interesting to take a glance at some of the reasons which were advanced by the enthusiastic Principal in favour of the proposed College. A few quotations from his pamphlets will best serve the purpose.

Writing in 1883 he had said:

Visions Again.

"As missionaries of a progressive Church which has always believed in schools and colleges, encouraging in the most practical manner every effort for furthering the cause of education, we cannot but feel concerned for the converts God is giving us in India, which shall be the means, in God's hands, of advancing the interests of His kingdom here. We would not be content to have our converts and their children remain on the same low level of intelligence where the Gospel found them. We wish for them growth, advancement, success, and one of the wisest methods for insuring these is to build up good schools whose uplifting influence shall be felt in years to come."

In the same pamphlet was struck a note which still resounds in the air, and promises to win more love and admiration for the College than perhaps any other one thing.

"The Christian College," he wrote, "like similar institutions at home, will also be of assistance to our Theological Seminary. By giving our young men a thorough education before sending them to the Theological school, we shall render both them and India Methodism valuable service. Our work demands educated native preachers, and this demand will be more keenly felt every year. In towns and villages much of the work can be done by those whose scholastic attainments are not high—earnest, humble workers, labouring among their own relatives; but in our city work and in our various appointments we must have well educated helpers, able to answer the numerous, and often difficult, objections which our opponents bring forward. Out of the 150 native preachers now employed (this refers to the year 1883) in the North India Conference, only *one* has passed the Calcutta University Entrance Examination, (Matriculation) a fact which speaks for itself, and a very strong argument in favour of a well-organized Christian College. Several of the most promising students now attending the Centennial School are planning to enter the Theological Seminary at Bareilly, and this number no doubt will be larger year by year."

The number *has* increased, and as a confirmation of the above statement, made twenty-three years ago, it may be said that there are at present writing twenty-four young men in the College and High School who have declared their intention of entering the Christian Ministry.

Writing under the date of 1885, Dr. Badley made the following interesting and striking statement :—

"American Protestants have given four Colleges to the Turkish Empire: Robert College at Constantinople; the Central Turkey College at Aintab; the Syrian College at Beirut; and the Armenian College at Hartpoot. American Missionaries of various denominations have been labouring in India for upwards of seventy years; the first College representing American liberality is yet to be established. In Calcutta, Madras, Bombay, and elsewhere there are large Colleges attended by 1,000 students each, all modelled after Dr. Duff's famous institutions at Calcutta, which have had an indescribable influence for good; but all these institutions are connected with English and Scotch Churches. America seems to have been left strangely behind; and yet so far back as 1819 when the Rev. William Ward, one of the famous trio of Baptist Missionaries at Serampore, visited America he secured $ 10,000 for the Serampore College. There are many reasons way Methodism should take the lead in educational matters; and surely the shortest way would be to raise a prosperous seminary to a college grade."

In making a contrast between the educational progress of our Church in India and on the other hand in China and Japan, Dr. Badley said:—

"Our Church is devising liberal things in educational matters in other foreign mission fields. The Anglo-Chinese College at Foochow, the Fowler University (named after Bishop Fowler) at Kiukiang, and the Anglo-Japanese College at Tokio are happy illustrations of this progressive, far-seeing spirit. Our plea is that India, the birth-place of religions, the home of philosophers, may not be longer overlooked; we have here a vastly larger population than Japan, a people much more accessible than those in China, and an English Government appreciative and helpful; no more promising field for educational work can be anywhere found to-day than India. The opportunity is inviting and promising beyond description; we cannot afford to let it pass unimproved."

The man who wrote thus of such a work was not to be disheartened by delays and disappointments. But such things were in store. In 1882 when the Rev. J. M. Reid, D.D., Secretary of the Missionary Society of our Church, visited India, Lucknow was one of the cities where he looked into mission work. He was much interested in the work of the Centennial School, and intimated that at no distant date he might aid in providing the institution with a new building. This word of Dr. Reid's was not forgotten, and was especially laid to heart by the Principal of the institution. For the next five years he kept in close touch with Dr. Reid, keeping up as steady a correspondence with him as Dr. Reid's time and inclination would permit. In two or three years he had made a sufficient impression upon this Missionary Secretary to elicit from him the following statement, which we find in a letter under date of August 19, 1885:—

"I cannot tell you how this enterprise of yours enlarges upon my mind month by month. I begin to get the thought which I know has been yours for a long time, that this institution (the 'Centennial High School') ought to rise to the rank of a college."

Such encouraging words it may be easily imagined, were not allowed to go by unimproved by the Principal. He continued the correspondence, urging upon Dr. Reid the rare opportunity of making the long talked-of College possible. Indeed we are forced to smile when we read in a letter from Dr. Reid, dated March 30, 1886, "I perceive you take most hopeful views of every encouraging word." That was it exactly, and a man with less hope would have abandoned Dr. Reid as a giver to the cause. Under date of May 1st, 1886, Dr. Reid sent the following discouraging words:—

"I have utterly abandoned the College project, so far as it depends upon my giving anything this year, beyond providing for the purchase of the land as already indicated by telegraph and letter."

The land referred to was a small plot adjoining the rear of the High School property. When the opportunity of buying this came Dr. Badley put a strong plea before Dr. Reid that it might be added to the School property being a most valuable and desirable piece of land. This Dr. Reid, as Missionary Secretary, agreed to do, advancing $ 2,500 personally, with the expectation of receiving it back at the hands of the General Missionary Committee. The same letter contains the statement that if he should have to make this gift of land a *personal* one, he did not intend to do any thing more for the College, a statement which makes us realize that his conception of the College enterprise had not yet reached the high place to which the

Principal of the school was steadily trying to bring it.

More cannot here be quoted from the long correspondence between Dr. Reid and Dr. Badley. A perusal of it makes the reader sensible of a steady, unchanging hope and purpose in the letters of the latter which are by no means to be found in those of the former. The outcome of it was that after many vacillations Dr. Reid did, in 1892, send $ 5,000 to which he later on added $ 10,000, the amount going for the erection of the present College building which was begun nearly a year before this gift came.

It was in 1885 that the Principal had the joy of fulfilling his vision of 1879 by building the Principal's residence on the rising ground to the East of the High School building. The other vision of the College building still lacked fulfilment; but it too was to be fulfilled, for the vision was founded upon unfailing faith in God and an undying devotion.

CHAPTER VIII

Overcoming Difficulties.

A College without buildings is better than no College at all, and if the name is once secured the buildings will, in all probability, come in due time. So thought the Principal of the Centennial High School. With this thought Dr. Badley used all possible influence, and during the session of the Annual Conference of 1887 was instrumental in having the following resolution passed :—

"In accordance with our Conference action in 1866, providing for the establishment of a mission college at Lucknow, the Board of Trustees of the Centennial High School, Lucknow, are authorised to raise the said school to a college grade this year by securing affiliation with the Calcutta University, provided the necessary financial help is secured from America or elsewhere."

Those on the field were not the only persons who were awake to the position the school had attained, and the career of greatness which seemed to be before it. The Principal had been indefatigable in his efforts to secure for it both friends and kind words. He let no opportunity slip to show the school and its workings to eminent visitors from America and elsewhere. Bishop Hurst, who visited the institution in 1885, wrote of it as follows :—

"I have visited the Centennial High School under the supervision of the North India Conference, and situated at Lucknow. It gives me great pleasure to say from what I have seen of the work done by the students, that I believe it to be one of the most successful and promising of all our Institutions in India. .. ... I commend this important school to the sympathy and generosity of our people everywhere, as being worthy of their love and liberal contributions. I hope the day is very near at hand when all the money needed for the complete endowment and full establishment of this school will be in hand. Its work is beyond all criticism. But it can do still better work, with larger means at command. Let help come promptly and in full measure."

Two years later Bishop Ninde, who visited India in 1887, wrote of the school in the following words :—

"No school I have visited in India has pleased me more than the Centennial

High School in Lucknow. It is wisely located in the chief city of Upper India. The vigorous yet judicious management of the Principal, Rev. B. H. Badley, M. A., has given the school a fine reputation, and it is a real credit to our Mission. The movement to advance it to the grade of a college has my cordial sympathy."

About the same time Bishop Warren, writing to Dr. Badley, said :—

Colleges are rising here that demand aid, but I think no one is so much needed as yours."

Bishop Newman added his testimony in the following words :—

"Our Church must awake to the fact that a Christian College in India is necessary to hold the Hindoo manhood for Christ."

But something more was needed than expressions of sympathy. During 1887 funds to make the opening of the College possible were not sufficient for the purpose. The original endowment for the Centennary College, which in 1867 had been reported as Rs. 10,000 and which by 1875 had amounted, as we have seen, to some Rs. 17,000, had ten years later " through judicious management " reached the sum of Rs. 26,000. This money could not, however, be taken for either building purposes or current expenses. It thus transpired that the permission to open the College which was granted in 1887 could not be taken advantage of until 1888. In this latter year on July 2nd the "Lucknow Christian College" was declared open and was ready to enroll students. Its affiliation at first was only up to the Intermediate or F. A. The affiliation to the B. A. came in 1889, although for lack of room no students could be taken in the two higher classes until 1891. The attendance the first year was naturally small, being limited to F. A. students. The Principal's report for the next year opens with the following statement :—

"The growth of a newly established College, receiving no grant-in-aid from Government and with no buildings of its own, must necessarily be slow. While fine buildings cannot make a college, all will readily admit that it is difficult to carry on college work in an ordinary school building filled with several hundred students of all grades, especially with the noise found in nearly all Indian schools. The teaching in our college during the year has been under special difficulties, and it is not to be wondered at that students prefer to go where they will not be crowded and where distracting sounds are absent."

Yet under these difficulties the work of the College had to be carried on for four years, the students' dormitories and the Principal's residence both being called into requisition to help out in the emergency.

It was useless, however, to think of a college building until a site had been secured for its erection. During 1887 and 1888 this was the chief concern of the Principal and friends of the College. If a site could only be secured, a strong plea could be made for the edifice. After many fruitless efforts there came at last the memorable occasion when the right thing was said and the right thing done. An account of this incident in the words of the venerable, Rev. T. S. Johnson, M. D., who was at the time Presiding Elder of the Oudh District, will be appreciated. From a letter received from him by the writer only this year, the following extract is taken:—

"We were debating the question of

location when your father said to this effect—'The thing to do is to go to Government and ask for that triangle of land; it is where the College ought to be located, and posterity will bless us for building it there.' This is about what he said. I arranged with him to go next day to see the Secretary to Government. Dr. Badley came to our house (now known as 'Dilaram' in 'Inayat Bagh') and he, Mrs. Johnson, myself and a lady who was staying with us,—Miss Millett knelt in prayer. Each one of the four prayed one after the other, after which we drove to the Secretary's office. Sir John Woodburn (afterwards Lieutenant-Governor of Bengal) received us and our request as though he expected us and wanted to comply with our request. He took the Lieutenant-Governor that evening to see the land and explained to him what we wanted it for. Certainly the Lord directed it all."

The triangle of land referred to in this interesting account by Dr. Johnson is the one opposite the High School on which the College building now stands. It was valued by the Government in those days at about Rs. 12,000, but must be worth to-day not less than Rs. 25,000, nor would the College be willing to part with it for Rs. 100,000. It is for our purposes invaluable. It is a site adjacent to the High School and the one which would naturally suggest itself as the most suitable, but there was no money wherewith to purchase it, and it needed the man who had the faith to ask for it as a gift! Dr. Badley in his Report refers to the incident as follows :

" We despaired of buying it, went to our knees about it, presented our application and in less than a month received a reply that the land would be given to the Mission 'free of cost and free of rent'—provided we erect our College building before a certain date."

But back of this brief reference to the subject there is a most interesting history, relating how the Principal came to propose that they ask for the site. What follows is quoted from a letter written by Mrs. Badley on the subject :

" All the time, that triangle of ground with the great tank gaping from the centre lay before us day by day. Donkeys grazed on the dry stubble ; a crop of mustard or a forest of castor bean trees grew upon it; stagnant water lay in the bottom, and goats climbed up and down the sides ; *dhobies* washed their few dirty clothes in it, and beggars sat under the trees along the edge and called aloud for *bakshish.*

"Your father always got up at half past four and spent a half hour in private prayer in his study. One morning when I came out he smiled and said, 'I have found a site for the College!' I said 'Where?' The night before, both he and Dr. Johnson had been greatly discouraged about it, and I was surprised. He answered—'It is the triangle across the road with the tank in it.' I laughed and said, 'What makes you say that?' And he said, 'When I knelt to pray this morning, I told the Lord that we must find a site for the College, and asked Him to direct me to the proper place and make it clear to me.' He went on to say that while his eyes were closed and his head bowed in his hands, that triangle across the road with its great tank gaping up at him, seemed to lie right under his eyes. He arose without praying another word, and went to the front verandah and looked across the road at the open space, and said out loud, 'I thank Thee, Lord,' and walked over to Dr. Johnson's and told him. They walked back and stood by the tank, and Dr. Johnson said, 'What can we do with this?' (indicating the tank). Your father answered, 'As I saw it when I prayed that question came to me, and the answer came, *fill it in.*'

The work of filling up the great, unsightly tank was begun by getting permission from the Municipal Board to have the city sweepings emptied into it, and the work was completed a few years later under the superintendence of Dr. Parker and Rev. Ganga Nath.

The condition on which the land was given was that a College building to cost not less than fifty thousand rupees, the plans of which the Government should first approve, be erected on the site within two years. The remarkable success in securing a site was looked upon as providential and spurred on to further efforts all who were connected with and working for the College. Of those outside the College, no one was more deeply concerned in the College enterprise or showed a more lively interest in it than Dr. Johnson. The Principal and he were in constant consultation and correspondence over the great project.

To those who know of the College enterprise only from without, Dr. Johnson was merely Presiding Elder of the Oudh District, and showed a natural and becoming interest in an institution thus taking shape within his own District and in his station.

But those who are intimate with all the facts, see in him one who was devoted heart and soul to the undertaking, who prayed for it and toiled for it, doing every thing he could to further its interests. He was a blessing to the institution in those early difficult years, and a close, sympathetic friend of the enterprise at a time when help and sympathy were most needed. His interest in the enterprise was altogether beyond that ordinarily to be expected from one who had merely an ecclesiastical tie to an institution within the area of his supervision.

Another rare friend of the College during these years of infancy was Rev. (afterwards Bishop) E. W. Parker, D. D. He was at that time Presiding Elder of the Moradabad District, but he was a man whose breadth of vision and sympathy made him a strong friend of the struggling, young College. He was at the time himself building up the Moradabad High School, (which now bears his name) and he knew what a stronghold for Christianity a truly Christain school or College could become. As President of the

Board of Trustees of the College at the time, he was in constant correspondence with Dr. Badley over the affairs of the College. Parker and Badley made a strong combination for any work. They wrought mightily for the glory of God here below and are doubtless being still more gloriously used in His Upper Sanctuary.

Although the money for the College building was not in sight, the next step was to get the official sanction of the Conference for the erection of such a building as had been specified by Government along with the gift of the land. This sanction was granted by the Conference of 1889. The following entry is found in the Report of the College published in 1889:

"The North India Conference at its recent session in Bareilly, (Bishop Thoburn presiding) granted the request of the Board of Trustees and sanctioned the immediate erection of the College building. It is thought that Rs. 10,000 can be secured in India from the Government and friends of education: for the remainder our eyes are turned to America, the land of Colleges, Churches and large-hearted Christians."

Overcoming Difficulties.

This action of the Conference in sanctioning the immediate erection of the building was due probably more to the enthusiasm and hopefulness of the Principal than to anything else. It was in perfect keeping with what he thought was the wisest course. The money was not in hand but the faith was there which would bring the money. When Dr. Badley reached Lucknow after that Conference he was as exuberant as a schoolboy ; he flung his hat up as high as the ceiling and shouted, "Hurrah for the College." Plans for the edifice were immediately drawn up. In the report of the College the Principal has the following words on the subject :—

"The plan for the proposed building, as designed by the Board of Trustees, has been approved by the Government, and it is hoped that work on the building may be commenced early in 1889, so that it may be finished by the end of the year."

Every effort was made during this year and the next to secure the needed funds for the College building. During 1889-1890 Rev. D. W. Thomas was acting as Agent for the College in

America, and in 1890 when Dr. Johnson went home on a short, necessary furlough, he too was armed with the powers of an Official Agent. During the same year Bishop Thoburn also solicited funds at home. All these attempts, however, were ineffectual in getting such a sum as was needed. At one time in 1890 it was even proposed by Bishop Parker and Dr. Thomas that Dr. Badley go home for the special purpose of raising money for the College. This, however, was not found praticable to attempt.

It is to be regretted that the building was not undertaken at once. Much to the disappointment of the Principal, when funds did not come in as fast as was anticipated, the Conference postponed the day of beginning operations. Dr. Badley's faith and plea were that the money would come and that the much-needed building should not be delayed; but the "Building Committee" which had been appointed, was instructed not to begin operations, "until the money was in sight." This was a sure and cautious enough policy, but it cost the

College two years of delay when a little less caution, a little more business sagacity and especially more practical faith in Him who had blessed the work of the College hitherto, might have saved the College a loss of two years, a loss irreparable from many points of view. Had it not been for the kindness on the part of Government in extending the period allowed for the erection of the building, the mission would have lost the valuable but conditional gift of land. It is instructive to note that the Woman's College of the same city, which now bears the loved and honoured name of Isabella Thoburn, was at this same time facing the same financial problem. When, however, the necessity became apparent Miss Thoburn borrowed the money and put up the indispensable College building. Subsequent years have amply justified her policy, and vindicated her faith.

However, in 1891, an agreement was finally arrived at with Dr. Reid which opened the way for the building to be begun. He at length proposed to pay $15,000 on the annuity plan, the money to be committed to the hands of three responsible men, who were to see it applied to the object for which it was given; the payments to draw 6% interest from date. This offer was accepted, the necessary papers were drawn up and signed, and with the money in sight, the work on the new College building was begun. Subsequently, however, Dr. Reid withdrew the condition which required the payment of an annuity, and made the money an outright gift. The difficulties had all been surmounted.

CHAPTER IX.

The Lucknow Christian College.

An American College, built on Indian soil, under the protection of the British flag, attended by Indian students, following the English system of education and supported by American money, is a College which cannot but be interesting. Such is the Lucknow Christian College.

The College dates from the year 1888, but until 1891 there was nothing to show to the passer-by. But thirteen years from the date when Dr. Badley was first appointed Principal of the infant Centennial School at the close of its first year, he was to have the joy of seeing the long talked-of, long dreamed-of College prepare to enter a permanent, a suitable home. It was doubtless with exultation he wrote the following sentence in the College Report published at the beginning of 1891—"The great event of the year—hailed with joy by teachers and students alike—occurring on the 18th of March, was the marking out of the foundation of the new building and beginning work thereon." An edifice, which is still an ornament to the famous city of Lucknow, was at last to house the first College of the Methodist Episcopal Church in Southern Asia.

But the College was much more than the building, and was well devoloped and in perfect running order before the days of a special building. It had more than a year before attained to the dignity of having two missionaries connected with it. In December 1889, in the person of the Rev. W. A. Mansell, M. A., S. T. B., it received and added to its Faculty its first regularly appointed Professor from home. The College Report for the year 1889-90 includes the following paragraph:—

"In December last we are happy to welcome to our teaching staff the Rev. W. A. Mansell, M. A., S. T. B., an experienced teacher. Mr. Mansell is a graduate of the Ohio Wesleyan University of Delaware, Ohio, and is supported by the students of the University, a practical expression of their interest in missionary work among the young men of India. We congratulate this noble body of students for their zeal and liberality, and trust that some other great literary

Institution in America may place our College under a similar obligation by sending us another teacher."

It is a matter for congratulation that the founder and first Principal of the Lucknow Christian College was a man of broad vision and of wide sympathy and experience. He was himself a man of deep scholarship and thorough culture, being the valedictorian of his class in College, and a man of studious and literary habits. Along with this he possessed a fervent spirit of evangelism which especially fitted him for so much responsibility in an institution composed of boys and young men. It is a great pleasure to notice the broad views taken of the activities of the newly established College. In the Report for 1890-91, he says:—

"Our institution is for all the Churches, not for a single denomination, it is 'the Lucknow Christian College.' We expect to enroll European as well as native students; our aim is to make the influence of the institution as far-reaching as possible."

In the Report published the year before, he spoke as a true missionary:—

Making a Christian College.

"We bespeak for this institution the co-operation of our missionaries in North India, and the sympathy and prayers of all Christian workers that it may be not only an educational centre but a successful evangelizing agency, by means of which many precious souls may find their way into the kingdom of God."

The desire to make the College reach as wide a constituency as possible accounts for the following announcement in the Annual Report of 1889-90:—

"Arrangements will be made for receiving European students, young men who have passed the Entrance Examination and desire to pursue a Collegiate course of study; such students will find ample opportunity for engaging in missionary work during their residence in Lucknow, so far as they may have leisure. Our aim is to build up an institution which shall not only advance the interests of the native Church but which may also be utilized by European students."

Ample provision was also made for mental culture, over and above what the class-room can ever be expected to give. Near the close of the year 1890-91 a Literary Society was organized, and a course of lectures on secular subjects, instituted some time previously, was successfully carried on. In addition to this a telescope, which had been secured some years before, was doing its share to add culture and breadth to the students. It is described by the Principal as "the largest in North India," and he goes on to say that it "will be an object of great interest to the students and to thousands of others, and will materially help in breaking down the erroneous opinions and fancies of the heathen people about us. We must now have an observatory."

As to a library, the foundation of that had been laid years before, and a constant endeavour was made to add to it.

But in the effort to provide adequately for the religious and mental life, the physical side of the student was not overlooked. Himself a keen lover of sports and enthusiastic about them, Dr. Badley did his utmost to make ample provision for the physical welfare of the students. He says in his Report for 1890-91 :—

"Counting the boarders (and foundationers) as especially committed to our care, not for a month but perchance for ten years, we desire their physical development; and to this end have spent and expect to spend money. As soon as we can afford it we expect to employ a military drillmaster and give our boarders the benefit of this form of exercise. By and by the gymnasium!"

Surely here was a wide view of the needs and all round development of each student. The secret of it lay in the ambition expressed in his last annual report: "We are labouring and planning to make the institution worth attending."

This brief summary of the aims and objects of the College is given in order to afford a view of the scope of the institution as seen by the founder. A good beginning was made in every department wherein lie the legitimate activities of a Christian College. The founder inaugurated the work, but left it for those who were to follow him to develop it along the fundamental and indispensable lines laid down, handing down for constant remembrance the motto of the College—"All to the Glory of God."

It was not until August of the year 1891 that a suitable opportunity was found for the laying of the foundation stone of the new College building. The following invitation was then issued, and as a result brought together on the occasion a very large assembly :—

"You are cordially invited to be present at the laying of the foundation stone of the Lucknow Christian College, at the College grounds, Golaganj, on Thursday morning, August 6, 1891, at 7 o'clock. The ceremony will be conducted by Bishop Thoburn." The programme used on that memorable occasion is given below in full :—

Lucknow Christian College

Laying of Foundation Stone.

August 6th, 1891.

1. Singing. . . . . By students' Choir- Hymn No. 16, Methodist Hymnal.
2. Prayer. . . . . By Rev Dr. Parker.
3. Brief Report of School and College. By Professor W. A. Mansell, M. A.
4. Address. . . . . By Bishop Thoburn.
5. Singing. . . . . Hymn No. 866, Methodist Hymnal : Tune—Duke

6. Depositing Box, and Declaring Contents. By Rev. Dr. Waugh.

7. Laying Corner Stone. . . . . By Bishop Thoburn.

8. Singing, Hindustani Bhajan. "Yisu Nama" By the Students' Choir.

9. Benediction.

A space had been left in the wall just to the right of the main entrance, and the stone was ready for the occasion, together with a box containing newspapers, including copies of the *Indian Witness* and *Kaukab-i-Hind* and other appropriate articles. A select choir of students from the two Colleges furnished the music, all who were present joining in singing the magnificent hymn by Professor Winchester so appropriate to the solemn occasion. "As we joined in the fifth stanza," says one who was present, "all hearts seemed awed and melted, as though it were a prayer and a prophecy." It will be recalled that eight years before the same grand hymn had rung out on the air when was laid the foundation stone of the Centennial High School just across the road, whose clock after all these years of steady, plodding at last indicated the hour for the laying of the foundation stone of the College building, and the bell sounded forth the seven steady strokes with a tone of triumph in its stately, majestic air. "To those present," writes Rev. W. A. Mansell in the College Report the next year, "who had seen the beginning of the Mission in Lucknow, and the first two or three orphan children taken in to receive the rudiments of an education, the sight was one which was the token of mighty victories already won, and the inspiration of achievements still greater soon to be realized." The stone, which was laid according to the ritual of the Methodist Episcopal Church, bears the following inscription:—

LUCKNOW CHRISTIAN COLLEGE

OF THE

METHODIST EPISCOPAL CHURCH.

THIS FOUNDATION STONE WAS LAID BY BISHOP J. M. THOBURN, AUGUST, 6TH, 1891.

And thus was laid the foundation stone of a Christian College on land which had once been a battle-field. During that very month, thirty-four years before, the site of the College had been occupied by the Sepoy rebels in besieging the Europeans beleaguered in the adjoining *Residency*. Over this site where Christian hymns now resounded there had been the shriek of shells and the whistling of bullets fired in fanatical fury at all who professed the name of Christ. Is there not significance in the transformation, or was it a mere *coincidence* that our missionaries entered the torn and bleeding city the very year after the Mutiny had been quelled?

A brief description of the building taken from the College Report for the succeeding year will give a good idea of what a valuable acquisition it was to the College and the Mission also :

"It is large, well-ventilated, and admirably adapted for the purpose for which it is intended. It will be hard to find a school building in India which equals it in attractiveness and convenience. In form it is a square, two-storey structure, flat-roofed and surmounted by an ornamental parapet with an airy and beautiful tower at the front right-hand corner. The building is almost entirely surrounded by a two storey verandah which, with its arches and artistic finish, greatly enhances the beauty and attractiveness of the whole. The main hall with its two wings will seat about seven hundred. . . . This room will be utilized for the daily chapel services, the regular College lectures and general addresses. The value of such a hall for direct missionary effort can hardly be over-estimated. In addition to the Chapel, the first storey contains the Principal's office, a Chemical and Physical laboratory and lecture-room (a library and reading room) and four recitation rooms. The upper story is devoted to recitation and lecture rooms."

The Lucknow Christian College had been established and a permanent home of beauty had been provided for it, but on the great day when the foundation stone of the new building was laid, where was the man to whose ceaseless efforts for the last thirteen years this memorable occasion and these stately walls were largely due ? To be absent on an occasion, such as this, was to Dr. Badley a matter of keen regret and great disappointment. Yet it only recalled to his mind how eight years before on another occasion of happy triumph he had been compelled to be absent on furlough. He had done the work but the joy of standing before his brethren on the day of days was not to be his either in 1883 when the foundation stone of the High School was laid, or in 1891 when was laid that of the College building. Nevertheless he was present in spirit, and was represented by a letter which was addressed to the Chairman of the meeting and the Lucknow friends. The closing words of the letter, which briefly reviewed the history of the institution, may be reproduced as especially significant: "As Missionaries we expect the day to come when we shall have Christian students enough to fill these College halls. ....The rapid growth of our own Mission assures us of this. The general desire for an education on the part of our converts' children speaks well for the future. Our doors are open to other classes—and to these we say, 'Come with us and we will do you good.' May the blessing of God continue to rest upon the Lucknow Christian College. May it be an honour to this great literary centre, Lucknow ; may it be a surprise and a joy to the Home Church which has planted it, an ornament and glory to the Native Church it especially represents : may its friends, already numerous, be greatly multiplied : and as years come and go, and young men, seekers after truth, followers of the right flock to these halls may they find light in Him who is the light of the world and walk rejoicingly in His presence."

The latter part of the year 1891 was spent by Dr. Badley in the hills whither he had been ordered by the doctor. The year preceding it the same thing had been necessary, and it was becoming apparent to all that he had not long to live. August 6th, 1891, found him in beautiful Almora, within four months of his victorious end, yet almost unconsciously preparing himself for the more beautiful paradise above. Those were days of patient suffering, but his weary head was already wearing the unfading crown of victory, and there came to him from time to time during the last months, from those whom he admired and honoured, messages which went like a soothing balm to his heart. About eighteen months before, when Dr. Badley had seemed to fail in strength and then had rallied again, Bishop, then Dr. Parker, wrote to him saying, "I am so thankful that you are better. I am willing to sit up nights and praise the Lord to see you better." A short time before this he had received a letter from Dr. Reid in which are found the following words:—"Your own sublime faith stirred my soul to its very depths, and I can see in the no distant future a veritable College as the result of your own labours and sacrifices." Labours and sacrifices had indeed been his, but his was a labour of love, and sacrifices most willingly, yea, rapturously made. With him at eventide it was light. To this eloquent testimony by these great men concerning the life and labour of the founder of the College, Dr. J. O. Peck added his in the following words:—"You are a glorious worker, one of God's heroes; and we love you dearly for yourself and your work's sake. Your work has enshrined you in the loving gratitude of the Missionary Society, and of a large number of the Church at home who have been kept advised of your devotion and noble service."

In a history of the College these few words find their proper place in helping to reveal the true worth of him who as its founder left nothing to the institution of more beauty and supreme worth than the example of his own life. No more could the history of the Isabella Thoburn College be written without dwelling upon the life and character of her whose loved name it bears, than can the history of our Christian College in Lucknow without reference to him who wrought his very life into this institution, and whose activity confronts us at every stage of its early progress.

CHAPTER X.

From Seventy-eight to Ninety-one.

The foundation stone of the new College building was laid on August 6th, 1891, and on November 20th of that year the man who had first been appointed Principal of the institution in 1878, since when he had laboured constantly in its behalf, was ushered into the presence of his Divine Master.

His labours were now ended. Nineteen years before he had landed in India, and of those nineteen years almost fourteen had been given to the institution under whose shadow he died. His hands and his mind had been busy with many other things as well as the College, but he had packed into those very years well-nigh a lifetime of strenuous exertion and heroic devotion in behalf of the institution for which he had chiefly lived. It will be very instructive and at the same time finely illustrative of the growth of the institution during the administration of its affairs by the founder to take a stock of its assets at the end of 1891.

The Rev. B. H. BADLEY, M.A., D.D.
Founder and First Principal of the College.

From Seventy-eight to Ninety-one.

First as to property. The College on the death of its first Principal possessed fourteen acres of land ideally situated even in a city of so many magnificent sites as Lucknow. This property at its present valuation is worth no less than Rs. 50,000, but the Board of Trustees would not take five times the amount in exchange for it. As to buildings, the little out-house had grown into two fine permanent structures for scholastic purposes, valued at Rs. 70,000; a large hostel for Christian boys costing about Rs. 15,000, and a Principal's residence put up at an expense of about Rs. 12,000. The total value of the building plant was therefore nearly Rs. 100,000. Leaving endowment out of the question altogether, the College had a valuable asset in the scholarships, temporary and permanent, which had been established through Dr. Badley's efforts. There were when he laid down the work eighteen permanent scholarships representing Rs. 28,000 from the interest of which amount eighteen students were being supported, and are still being supported. Of temporary scholarships there were thirty in force that year, representing nearly Rs. 3,000. Estimating from this the money which had, during the last ten years, come into the school in the shape of temporary scholarships, must have been nearly Rs. 25,000. Adding all these amounts together, we get Rs. 200,000 to represent the total money assets of the institution—exclusive of endowment.

The constituency of students which the institution had gained during these years is also worth considering. The total enrollment for the year 1891 shows 412, and for the fifteen years of the history of the institution the total attendance was over 4,000. The inspiration in the thought is that every student who had entered its doors had come within the influence of Christian teaching and high ideals altogether unparalleled by anything he had ever experienced before. Of the 412 enrolled in the year 1891, 49 were in the College Department—a very fine beginning, especially when we consider the fact that the College was but in its fourth year. As to other assets, which can be estimated, the good name of the institution should not be left unmentioned. It had secured for itself a host of friends in both India and America, had won the good opinion of all Government officials and established itself securely in the favour of the Indian Christian community, having made for itself in the hearts of the parents who were privileged to obtain its advantages for their sons a very warm place.

The Rev. W. A. Mansell, who succeeded Dr. Badley as Principal of the College, wrote as follows in the College Report in 1892:—

"The school has suffered a severe loss in the death of Rev. B. H. Badley, D. D., whose name has so long been associated with the school, and to whose efforts its present success is largely due. It is difficult to estimate the value of the work done by Dr. Badley in establishing the College on its present broad foundation. He very early took up the idea of enlarging the scope of the Centennial School to that of a College, and spared no labour to increase the effectiveness of the school, so that it gained rapidly in numbers and became the leading school in Lucknow. The valuable and extensive site upon which the school and College buildings are erected were obtained through his foresight and wise policy. And the erection of the new College hall marks the completion of one more of his long-cherished plans. It was his dearest wish that he might live to see the College building completed. While the wish could not be realized in its entirety, yet he was cheered during his last illness in seeing the building nearing completion, and expressing his satisfaction at the progress of the work, he said he must leave the scene of his labours below and obey the summons to 'those upper fields.' We miss sadly the inspiration of his presence and counsel; and taking up with heavy hearts the work he has left us, we cannot but feel that it will be long before his place will be filled."

The work of this servant of God was finished, and he sleeps peacefully in the city where his life-work was wrought, in the land of his adoption. Ten years later there was laid to rest beside him the earthly tenement of Isabella Thoburn, the founder of the Woman's College of Lucknow which now bears her name. They who had toiled so long together in the same city, working out the same great problem in behalf of India's young manhood and womanhood now rest side by side. Here the sounds of the busy city are hushed, but over across the river there are two

From Seventy-eight to Ninety-one.

Colleges, resounding with the voices of happy student-life, which will ever hold sacred the names of Isabella Thoburn and Brenton Hamline Badley.

CHAPTER XI.

Sunshine and Shadow.

The College was fortunate in having, at the death of the founder and first Principal, a man on the field who could continue the work. The Rev. W. A. Mansell, who had arrived two years before and was at the time of Dr. Badley's death Vice-Principal, stepped in and assumed the burden and responsibility. At the annual session of the North India Conference, in January 1892, he was appointed Principal of the College. For this work Mr. Mansell's scholarly habits, fervent spirituality and rare spirit fitted him admirably. The work before him was unusually difficult. The College had indeed struggled to its feet, but it had yet to confront most serious problems, and had a reputation to establish which would either make or mar it. Yet there was no real danger that it would collapse, for he who had laid its foundations had also built too well for the institution to always need his presence.

Sunshine and Shadow.

The Principal's Report for the year 1892 makes the announcement that in December of the previous year a re-inforcement for the Staff of the College had arrived in the person of the Rev. G. C. Hewes, B S., S. T. B. Mr. Hewes came from DePauw University as a representative of the student body of that institution who had pledged themselves to support him. He came with special preparation for scientific work and was gladly appointed to teach the Science classes, helping out also in the teaching of the English Literature.

During the year 1892 the finishing touches were put on the new College building, and on the 31st of October of that year, the edifice was formally opened by Sir Auckland Colvin, K. G. M. G., K. C. S. I., C. I. E., Lieut.-Governor of the Provinces. A description of this interesting occasion is taken from the Principal's Report for that year :—

"The crowning event of the year, the formal opening of the College Hall by His Honor the Lieutenant-Governor of the Provinces, occurred on the 31st of October. The building had been completed some months before; but circumstances prevented the formal opening of the hall with appropriate ceremonies until that date. The occasion was an important one, and the attendance of the English residents, native nobility, and our Christian community, made a fine audience.

"The main hall, seated with durable benches, for about seven hundred persons, was beautifully decorated with English and American flags, palms and fresh cut flowers, and with its magnificent arches and stately proportions presented a fine appearance. Precisely at half past four the band struck up "God Save the Queen," announcing the arrival of the Lieutenant-Governor. He was received by the Trustees, led by Dr. Scott, the President of the Board, Kunwar Harnam Singh, and the Rev. T. Craven, and escorted to his seat on the platform under an arch formed by the graceful folds of two large flags. At the joining of the flags was a shield of blue bearing in gold letters the college motto, *Omnia ad Dei Gloriam.*

"The Lieutenant,-Governor in his address made a most beautiful and appropriate reference to the union of the two flags he saw about him, remarking that it expressed the close union of the two countries represented, which were one in purpose and aim as well as in race. He expressed his great pleasure in being present for three reasons, first, because he had been brought into close relations with the College authorities, having had the privilege of granting the site on which the college stood, and it gave him pleasure to state that the conditions of the grant had been scrupulously and amply fulfilled by the Trustees. Again, he stated that ever since his arrival in India he had witnessed with much satisfaction the aid which missionaries in general gave to the Government in educational and philanthropic enterprises. He mentioned in most favourable terms the efforts of the missionaries of the Methodist Episcopal Church, their consistent and large hearted philanthropy, and their widely beneficent plans for the improvement of the people at large. The hall was then declared open, and after the national anthem and a grand display of fireworks for the benefit of those outside who could not gain admission, the exercises of the afternoon came to a close and the visitors were shown over the new building."

It was in this year 1892 that the first Christian young man passed a University Examination from the College. This young man was Nathaniel Jordan, who in this year passed the F. A. or Intermediate Examination and two years later was successful in gaining the degree of B. A. He stands as the firstfruits, therefore, of our higher educational system. He later received also the degree of M. A., was Professor of English literature in his Alma Mater for two years and now is the efficient Head Master of the Bishop Parker Memorial High School at Moradabad. American Methodism is justly proud of Mr. Jordan, who is an object of pride to his Alma Mater and an ornament to the Indian Church which he has so conspicuously served.

The Principal's Report for the year 1892-93 has the following sentence in its opening paragraph :—

"A completed College building, the receiving of the money needed for its erection, so that it now stands without a dollar of debt ; the opening of a new department in the College with fair prospects of success, these are the special events of the year."

The first part of the above sentence refers, of course, to the gift of Dr. Reid, the last instalment of which was received in 1892 and applied in liquidating the debt on the building.

It was in February 1892 that Dr. Reid paid over to the Missionary Society $5,000 for the College. This was the first instalment on the $15,c00 which he had a year before agreed to give. At first he had preferred the annuity plan but later had made the gift unconditional. The uncertainty which from the beginning had attended the matter did not end, however, when the first $5,000 had been paid. The letter from Dr. J. O. Peck, then Corresponding Secretary of the Missionary Society, which accompanied the money, gave little hope of any further gifts. It is dated February 10th, 1892, and says :—

"Dr. Reid does not agree to give the other, $10,000 to the College. That matter is in his own pleasure for the future, but the $5,000 is secure, for it is now on its way to India."

However, before the end of the year Dr. Reid saw his way clear to do what he seems to have had in mind all along, in spite of appearances. When the money had been made over to the College, he wrote to Mr. Mansell, under date of October 10th, 1892, as follows :—

"I am glad indeed that at last the $15,000 has settled down to the Lucknow College, for which it has for some years been intended, and which it would have been a great grief to me had it gone elsewhere, either by my premature decease, or by inability to satisfy my requirements."

The gift was most gratefully acknowledged by Mr. Mansell, in terms which touched Dr. Reid's heart and brought from him the following response:—

"Such words of love and gratitude from you have repaid me many times for carrying out the plan *concocted* between myself and the now sainted Badley. I am sure he sees and rejoices in it all, and will rejoice yet more as it proceeds on to perfection."

The "new department" referred to in the latter part of that sentence concerns the establishment of the Department of Commercial Education or the "Business Department," as it was first designated.

The establishment of a Department of Commercial Education was a very important step in the history of the College. The Rev. E. W. Parker, D. D., then presiding Elder of the Oudh District with his residence

A Group of the first Christian Students of Reid Christian College, taken in 1893.
Rev. W. A. Mansell in the centre, standing on his left
Rev. G. C. Hewes, and on his right Rev. H. L. Roscoe.

in Lucknow, is the man who is regarded as the author of this new Department. At his suggestion the work was undertaken. It was an advance step, taken in the right direction, proving our Church to be possessed of wisely progressive institutions. Our College was, as a matter of fact, the pioneer in such work in North India. For ten years she stood alone in the work; but what she realized then is realized on every hand now, and schools for the imparting of a commercial education have been established in many centres throughout North India, some by other Missionary Societies and some by Government.

The Principal of the College seems himself to have had a lively realization of the great importance of the new departure. Mr. Mansell, in his Report for 1892-93, refers to the matter as follows:—

"Mr. H. L. Roscoe, graduate of the Chaffee's Phonographic Institute, arrived last February to join our staff, as Professor in the Business Department. It has long been our desire to make our College as widely useful as possible for our young men, preparing them for responsible and lucrative positions in all departments. To this end we have taken the field, first among mission colleges, to teach stenography, type-writing, and general business writing and accounts. It is too soon to measure the success of the enterprise: but we have seen enough of the progress of the students who have already enrolled in this department, to know that they are not behind the youth of America in their aptitude for these studies. We believe that in a few years we shall not be able to supply the demand for trained and responsible Christian clerks and accountants. Our Christians are rapidly taking high and responsible positions in Government and public service, and it is important that we should seize our opportunity and fill these places with men in the highest degree loyal to Christ and the Church. So we use every means of increasing the number of avenues of employment for our young men, and mean to make all count for the glory of God and the speedy triumph of the Kingdom."

The opening of this work under Mr. Roscoe was marked by great succees. At the end of the first year it was realized that the hopes which had been entertained were destined to be fulfilled.

Another event of very considerable

moment which occurred during the administration of Mr. Mansell, was the changing of the name of the College. The first allusion to this change is found in the minutes of the Board of Trustees. Under date of January 13, 1893, the following entry is found :—

"The question of changing the name of the college was brought forward and referred to the Executive Committee."

At a subsequent meeting of the Board of Trustees, held in Allahabad on the 24th of February, 1894, there was made a second and final reference to the matter. The record is as follows:—

"On motion of E. W. Parker the following resolution was adopted.

'Resolved that we submit to the Committee on Education of the Central Conference the proposal to change the name of the College from the Lucknow Christian College to Reid Christian College, the Committee to report with their recommendation to the Central Conference for action.'"

The Central Conference, which met that

same week in Allahabad, gave its approval and the change of name was effected. The records of the Central Conference refer to the matter in the following words:—

"At the request of the Trustees we recommend that in view of the long-continued, hearty and efficient interest in our India work on the part of the Rev. J. M. Reid, D. D., of New York, Honorary Corresponding Secretary of the Missionary Society, the name of the above institution be changed, and that it be known henceforth as the *Reid Christian College.*" *Extract from the report of the Committee on Education, adopted by the Central Conference at Allahabad, on Monday, February 26th, 1894.*

Rev. W. A. Mansell in the College Report for 1893-94, alludes to the subject thus :—

"It will be seen that we have a new name for the College, and our patrons will be interested to know that the name has been given at the instruction of the Central Conference in recognition of the substantial help which Dr. J. M. Reid, Honorary Corresponding Secretary of the Missionary Society has given from time to time to the College, and also in recognition of the valuable services which he gave to India. The name is a fitting memorial of a worthy man, and we believe that additional honor will come to the College under its new title. May it become a name of increasingly holy and blessed memories, reflecting additional honor both on the Church and the man who has already made it honorable by his own good deeds."

The proposal to change the name of the College was not unanimously supported by the Board of Trustees. The Principal himself was not in favour of the change. As the years have gone by the sentiment has grown that the change of name was not wise. In the day of small things, Dr. Reid's gift of fifteen thousand dollars seemed to call for some special recognition, but as a matter of fact, this money did not make either the College or the building possible. It did come at an opportune moment to provide for the expenses of the building after it had been begun, but that is all. However, there is no need to belittle Dr. Reid's most welcome gift in order to support the view that the change of name was not a wise measure.

Dr. Reid was in every way worthy of the honor conferred upon him by naming our first and only College for young men in

Southern Asia after him. Still he himself had expressed his own opinion on the subject some years previous by saying that he did not believe it best for institutions on the foreign field to bear the names of those who had such an official relation to the Missionary Society as did the Corresponding Secretary. In this opinion, it seems to the writer that Dr. Reid was right. But in addition to this, the name which was given to the College in the beginning was incapable of improvement. The name itself told what the College was and where it was located. The city of Lucknow is famous the world over, and in India itself is a city which for historic significance is unsurpassed. The name "Lucknow Christian College" meant very much indeed, whereas the name *Reid* is nothing in India or, indeed, elsewhere, except to a small circle of American Methodists. The College lost much by the exchange. The common remark of the tourist and visitor is—"Whoever this Reid was, this is a noble memorial to his name." For the institution to have stood as *the* Christian College of Lucknow and to have been known thus, would have meant much every way. If the name was changed in the secret hope of future bequests to the College the hope was doomed to disappointment. Syracuse University was the institution which claimed Dr. Reid's chief interest, and to it he made large donations. Ten years after his death his widow left $6,000 in her will for our College, but that was all the College received subsequent to the first gift. Writing at this distance, when the interested parties have all passed off the stage of action, the historian has felt that these few words would not be out of place or be misunderstood.

It was in 1894 that the College was privileged to extend a welcome to the Rev. D.L. Thoburn as an addition to the Faculty of the institution. The Report for that year refers to his arrival as follows :—

"We have great pleasure in announcing that our Staff has been very materially improved by the addition of the Rev. D.L. Thoburn, B.A. (of Allegheny, and S.T.B. (of Boston University). Mr. Thoburn is thoroughly accomplished and a teacher by instinct, and will no doubt add greatly to the efficiency of our work. He will have charge of the work in English Literature in the college."

Mr. Thoburn continued his work in the College until March 1st, 1896. It is a pity he could not longer have been associated with this work for which he was so strikingly fitted. The exigencies of the general work, however, required his services as Agent of the Methodist Publishing House, to which post accordingly he was appointed where he won fresh laurels for himself in a most difficult work. For the next nine years he was associated with that work, laying down his heavy burdens only last year when death removed him from the scene of his many labours.

The same school-year which saw the transfer of Mr. Thoburn to the work of the Press, was marked by two other serious losses to the College, the first being the departure to America of Mr. Roscoe whose health necessitated his leaving the country, and the second the transfer of Mr. Hewes. Thus in the course of a single school-year the institution lost three valuable men. Such a crippling of its teaching staff was most deplorable, and while partly due to unavoidable circumstances was due in some measure also to a narrow-minded policy regarding the College. The general feeling was that one missionary, or at the farthest two, would be quite sufficient to carry on the work; whereas such an institution can never do its work as it ought to without at least four missionaries on its staff. The future was, however, to see the adoption of a more liberal policy. There are serious disadvantages in having men on the Staff who are subject to appointment by a Conference, which naturally cannot consider the interests of the College only but must provide for the whole work, bearing in mind all its institutions and departments. The result is that the College has more than once suffered by losing men, by whose continuance in the work the best interests of the institution would have been served.

The departure of Mr. Roscoe who had so successfully guided the Department of Commercial Education through its first few uncertain years, left this important and growing Department without a Manager. This vacancy, however, was soon to be admirably filled in the person of Rev. J. N. West, M. A., S. T. B.

The College Report for 1895-96 makes the following reference to the subject :—

"We were fortunate in being able to secure (Rev.) J. N. West formerly of our Mission in Madras, as Professor in the College and Manager of the Business Department."

Mr. West's arrival was thus most opportune. He not only carried a full amount of work in the College proper, but took so kindly to the struggling, little Department of Commercial Education that, as we look back now upon that period, we are inclined to think its very existence depended upon his interest and labors in its behalf. Indeed, at one time when a suspension of the work of the Department was under consideration, it was Mr. West's offer of special attention to its needs that secured its continuance.

During the year 1896 the shadows gathered heavily over the young College. Not only was the existence of the Department of Commercial Education threatened, but the College itself was in danger of being reduced to the F. A. grade, a backward step which would have left it little better than an Academy. We tremble now to think that the proposal was ever made or that such a dangerous step, such a retrograde movement, was even discussed. There is no doubt that the circumstances were peculiarly discouraging, but it requires the supposition of a good deal of short-sightedness to account for the failure to see that a reduction of the College to the F. A. grade meant a blighting of all possible progress and foreshadowed, yea invited, another step backward.

The college reports do not say anything about the proposal to close the upper classes of the College. In fact the public never learnt how near the institution came to this great calamity. The only record to be found is in the minutes of the Board of Trustees. The matter was first brought up officially in 1895. Under date of March 26th of that year, the following entry is found:—

"The question of reducing the College to intermediate grade was brought forward and it was decided to make no reduction at present, the Principal to report on the subject again at the next annual meeting of the board at conference."

This next annual meeting was held at Bareilly on January 11th, 1896. At that time the following minute was recorded:—

"The matter of reducing the grade of the College to the intermediate standard was brought up, and on motion of D. L. Thoburn it was (decided) to take no action till after the close of the present school year"—*i. e.*, after May 1st, 1896.

This, as may be seen, was ominously indicative of an inclination on the part of some at least of the trustees to take the backward step. At a succeeding meeting, which was held that same year in the Methodist Publishing House at Lucknow, the matter came to a climax. To the historian of the institution that seems a terrible moment when the fate of the College hung, as it were, in the balance. True, the discontinuance of the B. A. classes did not necessarily imply the closing of the two lower classes also, but when the ground is uncertain under the feet, one wrong step makes another very easy.

However, the Board of Trustees of the College met, and the *pros* and *cons* of the question were again gone over. It would be interesting now to know how those eight or ten men ranged themselves in regard to this question. No record of that, however, remains. What we do know is that they were equally divided on the question, evidently four on one side and four on the other. The deciding vote was in the hand of the Chairman! Well was it for the College that the chair that day was occupied by that great and far-seeing man, Bishop (then Dr.) Parker. He had rendered many valuable services to the College, but none of them was more valuable than his service wisely rendered that day. One who was present at the meeting says, "Dr. Parker announced that the vote was a tie, and then with a characteristic turning of his head to one side, and a smile gathering on his lips he said: 'The casting vote lies with the chairman and he won't vote; so that settles it!'"

That did settle it, and the crisis once passed there never again came a time when there was any inclination to lose heart in the College enterprise. Considering the marvellous leading of the past and the altogether unmistakable signs of God's constant blessing upon the institution, it was not for a moment to be thought possible that what the Lord had so remarkably sustained through year of difficulty, and aided in its magnificent development from the feeblest beginnings He would now allow to suffer a declension. Praise God there were some who did not misinterpret God's providences or in the darkness lose the grip of confidence!

The proposal to reduce the grade of the College was not altogether without reasons. These may be briefly referred to. In the first place it will be remembered that those were years of unusual financial depression especially in the United States which is the direct source of the financial support of the College. Money from America came slowly in spite of all appeals, and the Missionary Society was compelled to cut down its appropriations in a way that was most keenly felt and regretted on the foreign field. In India itself, famine conditions had begun to prevail, and the immediate vicinity of the College itself was beginning to feel the effects. In the next place, students in the upper classes were few, and the fees realized were consequently small; whereas the maintaining of professors for these upper classes was a very expensive affair.

During 1896 when the reduction was under consideration, there were only twenty-two students in attendance, and most of these were in the two lower classes. Two or three years previous to this time there were many more students, but the large number had been due to an indiscriminate admission of nearly all who applied. The result of this was that the student-body had a large percentage of men who represented the most undesirable class of students. When they appeared for the University examinations they gave so poor an account of themselves that the reputation of the College suffered in consequence. The Report for the year 1893-94 shows that the College soon saw that to enroll students at such a cost was suicidal. The Report says:—

"We have not tried to increase the attendance, believing that it is better for the present we should continue to exercise some care in the admission of students. The number applying for admission is large, but mostly consists of those who have failed to gain admission to other Colleges. Owing to difficulties we have had to encounter in maintaining our Staff of Instructors, our examination results have not been very gratifying, and until we can show satisfactory results in examinations, we shall not have a large number of applications from the better and wealthier class of students."

In the years which immediately followed, the results of examinations were better, but the attendance decreased until, as has been stated, in 1896-97 it had dropped to only twenty-two. It is not surprising then to find those who looked only at the present, proposing to do away with the heavy expenses entailed by maintaining the B.A. department and to wait for a more favourable time to build it up. But the case was not such a bad one and called for no such serious measures. With the failure of the proposal and the continued exercise of faith and patience, the clouds lifted and the sunshine of God's blessing which had really been streaming down all the time was again apparent to all.

The same year which terminated Rev W. A. Mansell's connection with the College as its Principal was marked by the death of Dr. Reid. The following resolution which, under date of July 16th, 1896, was spread on the minutes of the Board of Trustees shows in what esteem Dr. Reid was held :—

"Resolved that we have heard with profound sorrow of the death of the Rev. John M. Reid, D.D., late Honorary Secretary of the Missionary Society of the Methodist Episcopal Church. In his death the Church has lost a faithful and honourable servant whose labours have been abundantly blessed in building up the Church he loved.

"He will long be honourably and affectionately remembered for his deep interest in the work in India during his incumbency as Corresponding Secretary of the Missionary Society. He has rendered signal service to the cause and Kingdom of Christ in this land, by giving the means for erecting a building for the Reid Christian College which will be a lasting memorial to his name and his loyal devotion to his Church.

"We would recommend that a suitable memorial tablet be placed in the Hall, setting forth in appropriate expression the salient parts of his life and his service for the Church in general, and especially in India.

"We would give expression to our sympathy with Mrs. Reid in her affliction, and pray that God may sustain and comfort her until the day of meeting again."

The sunshine was indeed accompanied by shadows during the five years of the College with which this chapter is concerned. But shadows are *due* to the sunlight. To those who realized this and were content to toil in deep shadows, not losing sight of the great Light, the College owes the profounder debt of gratitude.

CHAPTER XII.

Enlarging Visions.

An appointment to Reid Christian College in 1897 was not, ordinarily considered, an enviable one. An appointment, however, was made necessary by the departure of the Principal, Rev. W. A. Mansell, at the beginning of the year. Mr. Mansell, whose scholarship and eminent qualifications as a teacher had made him so valuable to the institution, still had a strong leaning towards and fitness for purely evangelistic work. The need, moreover, in that field was very great, and thus it came about that the Annual Session of the North India Conference held in January 1897 appointed him Presiding Elder of the Oudh District. As Lucknow was the head-quarters of the District, Mr. Mansell did not have to leave the City : indeed he continued throughout the year to give much time and attention to all College affairs.

The vacancy caused by Mr. Mansell's

transfer was filled by the appointment of the Rev. C. L. Bare, M.A, B.D., as Principal of the College. He came to the work with ripe scholarship, a rare sympathy with young people and an experience of seventeen years missionary life, during which time he had seen much of both evangelistic and educational work.

The College was still in the day of small things and had many of its battles yet to fight. The years of financial distress were not yet over, and the great Indian famine of 1897 was at its worst. The fair regions of the great Northern Indian plain were themselves a scene of desolation. The spectre of famine, gaunt and wild-eyed, stalked through fields, hamlets and cities, where millions who had only heard of his devestations now saw for themselves and, alas, *felt* also ! The City of Lucknow was full of starving, dying people. The College premises were invaded from morning to night by those who sought relief. They were given work, so far as possible, and foreign corn, straight from the generous hands of America, was doled out to all. Think of 3,000 people having but one consuming thought all day long, and that to get a handful or two of shelled corn ere the lengthening shadows merged into the darkness of night ! Men, women and children struggled over and contested every grain of the precious seed.

And the College ? Alas for the College, which drew its students chiefly from the poorer class ! Those were dark days for it. The Principal writing of the year says, "We have held our own in the face of difficulties." That was about all that could be said. The attendance for the school year was only twenty-two. The High School also had suffered, as much from unscrupulous rivals as anything else. The result of it all was that the total attendance in both College and High School was less than half what it had been six years before.

The new Principal, however, set to work both zealously and patiently. The College had now entered upon its tenth year, and a vantage-ground had been gained from which a wider vision was possible. A few years more of faithful toiling and the path would be clear to larger success. Mr. Bare began by voicing with redoubled energy the needs of the College. The necessary endowment was estimated at Rs. 600,000, while the sum of Rs. 500,000 was aimed at for the purpose of establishing scholarships. Special appeals were prepared and circulated. That these large sums were never actually realized is not to the point; it meant much to make an effort to get them and to realize that the School could use them. The necessity of a hostel for non-Christians was emphasized, and steps were even taken looking towards the opening of Law Classes in the College. A strong representation was made through the Board of Trustees to the Conference, urging the appointment of a larger number of missionaries for this great educational work. All this indicated an aggressive policy which was most hopeful, and though the day of "small things" was not gone, the day of larger things was in sight.

It was at this time that the historian's personal knowledge of the institution began. He arrived in India in December, 1899, and in January 1900 was appointed to a Chair in the College.

The new century brought with it a period of steady growth. It was still uphill work, but the College never failed to secure a reasonable return for all the effort expended. Though the students in the College of Liberal Arts numbered only thirty at the beginning of 1901 yet the time had come when there were to be no further fluctuations such as had marked past years. From that time on, an increase in attendance has been registered each year. The Department of Commercial Education welcomed the new century with a beaming face. Its growth had been sure and steady from the beginning. In 1901 there were on its roll seventy-five students, about two-thirds of whom were Christians. The demand for typists and stenographers still exceeded the supply, and no man who finished the course ever failed to get a post commanding a good salary.

But the first year of the new century brought also a great loss, alike to the eduational and the evangelistic work of our Church in North India. On June 4th, 1901, Bishop E. W. Parker ended his great career in Naini Tal, and on September 1st of the same year Miss Isabella Thoburn, Principal of the Woman's College at Lucknow, ceased at once to work and live. The death of these great leaders, especially that of Bishop Parker, touched the College very closely. At the time of his death Bishop Parker was President of the Board of Trustees of Reid Christian College. He had just returned from the United States after being elected to the Episcopate, and the College was looking toward him with special expectation. His residence had been fixed in Lucknow, and there was every hope that his great heart and head, ever resourceful in every good cause, would soon be busy in behalf of the College. But it was not so to be.

The Board of Trustees, which had a meeting on the very day of Bishop Parker's death, passed the following resolution:

"Whereas Bishop E. W. Parker, Chairman for many years of the Board of Trustees, has this day fallen asleep in Jesus, Therefore, resolved that we place on record our great appreciation of his long and memorable service as a missionary of over forty-two years, and our sense of great loss to this Board and to the College of which he has been a most devoted friend.

"Resolved, further, that we send a copy of these resolutions to Sister Parker and assure her of our sincere sympathy and prayers in this hour of great bereavement."

Up to the very day of his death Bishop Parker evinced a great interest in the College which he had so often helped and which had taken shape under his own eyes. From the founding of the College until his death he had served as a member of the Board of Trustees, during the latter period being Chairman of the Board. On his death there came to the College the greater part of his library, and also sufficient money to establish several scholarships. He believed most thoroughly in the great educational work of the Church in India.

The death of Miss Thoburn, while not touching the work of the College so closely, had yet a direct bearing upon it. Whether the work of the Church or school were considered, Lucknow with Miss Thoburn was what it could never be without her! The removal of a light which shone so clearly and conspicuously, the silencing of a voice which spoke with unfailing tenderness yet never compromised firmness, the vanishing of a personality which had made love real, sacrifice attractive, holiness practical, and illustrated in itself the most difficult teachings of Christianity, this was a loss almost beyond the possibility of realizing. Miss Thoburn's position as Principal of the Woman's College had brought her into close relations with the educational work as a whole, and in the Church, the Sunday School, the Epworth League and the Prayer Meeting her influence with the young men was just as great as it was with the girls of her own school. For years she taught a Sunday School class composed of the young men of the College, and for her to teach in the Sunday School was to reveal Christ by words which won their way to every heart, compelling interest, and through a personality which excited wonder and admiration the more it was studied. Her influence could no more be confined to Lal Bagh than can the sunlight be shut out from the earth. For years her presence in Lucknow was a priceless possession to Reid Christian College, and its power will be felt during all the years that lie ahead. The wisdom, zeal, love and patience with which she built up the great work of the Woman's College was always an inspiration, and very often a help, to those who were working out the same problem in behalf of the young manhood of our Church in India. These few words concerning Miss Thoburn's character and influence are written with deep conviction and great gratitude.

At the end of the year 1901 Mr. Bare's health was such as to require his taking a furlough to America, which accordingly was granted by the Annual Conference which met in January, 1902. In March of that same year he set sail with his family.

It must have been with a feeling of satisfaction that Mr. Bare handed over the work of the College to his successor. During his term of five years he had done much for the institution. In the first place, the confidence of the public had been secured. With a steady growth visible in all departments, people began to believe in the stability and prosperity of the institution. The popularity of the College was manifest and friends were rising up who did not hesitate to speak well of the institution. This was due in a good measure to the better results in the University Examinations. During the last two or three years these were sufficiently good to call forth kind words in many quarters where the success of a Christian College was anxiously watched. Finally the endowment fund of the College was left by Mr. Bare in good shape. During the last few years its increase though not rapid was steady. Scholarships, both permanent and temporary, had also increased, and while the finances of the institution left many things to be desired, yet there was much to be thankful for considering the years of famine and general financial distress which had so recently been experienced.

CHAPTER XIII.

Coming into Our Heritage.

The appointment of the Rev. J. N. West, M. A., S. T. B., to succeed Mr. Bare as Principal of Reid Christian College was very generally popular. For the last six years Mr. West had been in close touch with the affairs of the College, and was well fitted both by education and experience for this important position. He entered upon his labours in his new capacity with great enthusiasm. The College had now got the swing of victory; prosperity and progress were in the air. For several years the tide had been steadily rising and the new Principal was not the man to miss the opportunity of taking it at the flood. This the Conference had felt in appointing him to the place.

One of the very interesting events of the year 1902 was the founding of the Alumni Association of the College. Of this new departure, the Principal was the heart and soul. During the summer vacation of that

The Principals of the Institution. In 1888 it attained the rank of a College.

year, a sufficient number of old students happened to be in the beautiful hill station Naini-Tal, to make it possible for the Association to be organized. On the 26th of June some twenty-five alumni of the College and Department of Commercial Education gathered at the Mission Sanitarium for this special purpose. The occasion not only proved to be of great interest and pleasure, but the work of formally organizing the new body was most satisfactorily completed. Mr. J. Devadasan, B. A., was elected the first President and Mr. J. R. Chitambar, B. A., the first Secretary. Such is a brief record of the humble beginning of this very important branch of the college activities.

The years have brought an increasing interest to the annual meetings of the Alumni Association. Its existence has been a great help to the College, in its effort to foster an affection for the *Alma Mater* in the hearts of her sons. Such a bond between the College and its ever-increasing alumni had been a decided lack during all the years of its existence. A wise policy had at last supplied it, and the future only will be able to fully show the significance of the work done that day. Already, however, the meetings of this Association of "old boys" have been fraught with great good to the College and the student-body. An *esprit de corps*, a thing by no means indigenous to Indian schools and Colleges, and a slow grower even under the most favourable circumstances, is gradually making itself felt. Yet it must be admitted that non-Christians are very slow to make any response whatever. Probably for years to come the Christian students—themselves but beginners—will have to lead the way to more practical and whole-hearted loyalty.

The young Alumni Association of the College proved that its loyalty consisted of something more than mere words, by setting out to found an Alumni Scholarship in their *Alma Mater*. At the present writing more than one-third of the Rs. 1,500 required have been raised from various sources. A short time will probably see the completion of this laudable work, and as the alumni increase in numbers they can turn their attention to larger undertakings.

And thus in one way and another the College gained in reputation and standing. For many years most favourably regarded by its own constituency and community, it now began to extend the sphere of its influence. During Mr. West's administration of its affairs, the authorities of the College were approached by the Wesleyan Methodist Mission with a proposal looking to co-operation in this great educational work. It was suggested by the Wesleyans that they regularly appoint one of their own missionaries to serve on the Faculty, and, without assuming any further financial responsibility, regard the College as the proper place to send all their own young men who desired to pursue a College course of studies. This proposal was met with general approval by the College and its governing body. The way was opened up for further deliberation on the subject, but for some reason or other the project did not take shape. A hope may, however, be reasonably entertained that in the fulness of time such an idea will be carried out. Meantime, of course, the doors of our College are always wide open to young men of all denominations. In South India the plan of denominational co-operation has been working admirably for years, and the great Christian College at Madras has amply illustrated both the feasibility and desirability of such an arrangement.

Nothing during this period did more to bring the College prominently before the public, both in the United Provinces and elsewhere in North India, than the admirable work of the Department of Commercial Education. From the beginning of the work in 1893 it had been steadily growing in favour with all who knew anything of it, and gaining the gratitude of an ever-increasing body of young men who were desirous of fitting themselves for just such positions as those to which a course in the Commercial College led.

So signal was the success of this enterprise that in 1903 the Government of the Provinces itself became a patron. For some time past the Government had shown unusual interest in what was then considered a unique work, and at last decided to benefit by the existence of such an institution. Their first idea had been to open a similar School in Cawnpore for the training of their own clerks and employes, but on further consideration they decided to save, for the present at least, the heavy expense that would thus be entailed, and avail themselves of our own fully-equipped institution.

As a consequence, the Government of the United Provinces deputed seventy-four clerks to our College for a special course in typewriting. This was an unprecedented thing. They represented all the Judges', Collectors' and Deputy Commissioners' Offices in the Provinces, having been granted three months special leave for this work. At the request of the Government the College undertook the difficult work of training them in typewriting and guaranteeing a speed of at least thirty words per minute. Some very crude material was naturally sent in, and the time granted was less than half that ordinarily required, but all were successfully trained, the average rate of speed exceeding the requirement by five words per minute.

The success of this special work was due almost entirely to Mr. West's indefatigable efforts to give the best instruction and make the best of every hour. He rightly felt that the responsibility of having such a Government class was very great, and that on its being faithfully and satisfactorily discharged much depended. The annual report of the College for 1903-4, in referring to the subject, says :—

"Aside from our regular students in the Department, the Government deputed 74 clerks to us for special training. These young men completed their work and have gone back to their respective offices. That the experiment was a success, is attested by several things. We have not heard a single complaint made by any official as to the character of the work being done by any student trained by us. Another evidence is, that Government has asked us to take another deputation of clerks from another branch of Government. And last but by no means least, the Government has put a sanction upon our work by givivng us a grant of Rs. 1,500 for further equipment, and

Rs. 100 per mensem to increase our teaching staff."

It was only natural that the publicity given to the work of the Department of Commercial Education by such Government patronage, should help in bringing the institution, as a whole into the public eye. It was the best sort of an advertisement, and the College was throughout the centres of the Provinces a subject of favourable comment as never before.

At the end of the year 1903 Mr West, who had completed eleven years service as a missionary in India, was granted a furlough to America. His term of two years, brief as it was, had been marked by an administration both brilliant and judicious. The affairs of the institution generally were in good shape. The Christian Boarding House, in the welfare of which Mr. West had been particularly interested, gave ample witness to the careful attention which it had received. The attendance in every department of the institution had increased, and in January 1904, when Mr. West handed over the reins to his successor, the total enrolment showed the high-water mark of 527. This was made up as follows:—In the two affiliated High Schools, 341; in the Department of Commercial Education 144, and in the College of Liberal Arts 42.

Mr. West's work did not cease, however, when he set sail for America. While in that country, supposedly on furlough, he gave himself without stint to the work of soliciting funds for the College. For such work he was admirably fitted, as may be seen from the fact that during his furlough of less than two years, he succeeded in securing twenty-five temporary scholarships representing a value of Rs. 3,000, and five permanent scholarships representing Rs. 7,500. In addition to this, much was received in the way of miscellaneous gifts due to his advocacy of the needs of the College at home. But the institution which he loved so well and served so enthusiastically, did not need these sums of money to attest his continued interest. He who had given himself to its cause, could make no greater gift.

CHAPTER XIV.

The Day of Greater Things.

In this the closing chapter of this history of our Christian College at Lucknow, a glance must be taken at the events of the past two or three years, and an attempt be made to give an idea of the present condition of affairs.

In January 1904 Rev. C. L. Bare, after two years of successful advocacy in America of the needs of the College, took over the work from Rev. J. N. West who was bound home on furlough. It must have been a very great pleasure indeed for Mr. Bare to re-enter upon the work to which he had devoted five years of his previous term of service, and a satisfaction to find things in such a generally good condition. His heart was in this enterprise and he set about at once to give himself up to the great work.

In July 1904 the Staff of the College was reinforced by the arrival from New York City of Rev. T. C. Badley, who came as

Manager of the Department of Commercial Education. The work of this Department had so grown as to require the entire time of the man who was put in charge of it. For the last two years Mr. Badley, in spite of the fact that the added responsibility of the evangelistic work of our Lucknow Circuit has been his during this last year, has discharged the duties of the Manager of the Department of Commercial Education to the satisfaction of all concerned. The annual report of the College for 1904-5 says:—"The loss sustained by Mr. West's leave to America has been fully met by Mr. T. C. Badley's coming as Manager of the Department. He has been a great relief to an already overworked Staff. The Department under Mr. Badley has prospered in every way."

The Department of Commercial Education is at present experiencing keen competition, which has been largely the outcome of its own great success. Rival schools have been started in several centres of the Provinces by both Government and mission institutions, while in Lucknow itself two or three such schools are doing their utmost to get a footing, and are bidding freely for patronage. This rivalry has naturally told somewhat on the attendance, but there is still no school in the Provinces that holds the place ours does. When the rage for opening such schools has abated, and the supply of typists and stenographers corresponds more nearly to the demand, many of these rival schools will die a natural death, doubtless leaving us to pursue our own course.

It was in 1904 that the College was indebted to the Rev. G. W. Briggs, M. A., for several months of special work as a member of the Faculty of the College. In an emergency Mr. Briggs stepped in and taught in the Departments of both Mathematics and Political Economy. The arrangement was entirely satisfactory to the College, but Mr. Briggs' work in the English Church made it impossible to continue the plan. The year before, the Rev. P. S. Hyde, M. A., then Pastor of the Lal Bagh English Church, had similarly obliged the College by taking up work in the Department of English Literature

The Principal would have been very glad to have Mr. Hyde continue his work in the College, but here again the arrangement broke down because of the demands of the evangelistic work. These two cases only go to show that the College needed more men on its Staff in order adequately to provide for its increasing needs. It is with great pleasure the writer adds that, just as this book is going to press, word has come from America that a man has been appointed to the Science Department of the College. When Prof. Henry arrives, which it is hoped will be about Christmas time, he will find an important work awaiting him in a realm which is on the eve of a great *renaissance*. The East has heard the voice of science and is beginning to respond.

The year 1905 was one of the most critical and at the same time most significant years in the history of the institution. Two events must stand out prominently in any account of this period, and to these the historian now turns.

The Day of Greater Things.

Early in November 1905, the authorities of the College were greatly surprised one evening to find the College premises invaded by a most distinguished looking party. On going out the Principal found that His Honour, the Lieut.-Governor of the Provinces, Sir James Digges La Touche, K.C.S.I., with his Private Secretary, the District Engineer and others had come to see if the College property were indeed so desirable a site for the location of a great Medical College as they had reason to think. They went over the grounds, being most favourably impressed with the site and particularly with the commanding position of the High School building and the residence of the Principal. The party then took their leave evidently highly satisfied with their visit and what they had seen, but they left behind in the hearts of all who had any interest in the College a vague dread and a sense of approaching calamity.

It is necessary to go back and state that in anticipation of the visit of H. R. H. the Prince of Wales to India and to the chief centres of the United Provinces, the Indian public, led by the nobility of the Provinces, has proposed to Government that a Medical College to serve for the whole Province be established at Lucknow, and that the Prince of Wales be asked to lay the foundation stone. Government gave its assent, money for the new project poured in, and in an almost incredibly short time the proposed institution had about Rs. 600,000 in sight as a building fund. Within the space of six months one of the finest Medical Colleges in India was assured.

When it came to locating a Medical College in Lucknow, there were certain considerations which would naturally cause all eyes to be turned towards the site occupied by the Christian College. Among these was the fact of its central location. If Hosainabad on the extreme West be taken as one horn of a crescent and Husainganj on the extreme East be taken as the other horn, our College stands about midway between the two, while it is itself outside the densely populated parts. It is open on threesides to wind and sky, while on the South it faces the native city and the chief thoroughfare of Lucknow. For the location of any public building the city affords nothing better. Within half a mile are the world-renowned "Residency" grounds, the United Service Club housed in a royal palace, the Station Library, the fine Provincial Museum, the grand new High Court for all Oudh, the Central Telegraph Office, the imposing quadrangle of buildings called Kaisar Bagh which surrounds the beautiful public hall known as the *Baradari*, the City *Kacheri* housed in another palatial building of the days of Oudh's royalty, the proud dome of the tomb which marks the resting-place of one of Oudh's celebrated Mohammedan kings, the handsome building of the Canning College, the new imposing and exquisite marble memorial to the late Queen Victoria, the Lady Dufferin Hospital for Women and the Balrampore Hospital for the general public. There is not another such site in Lucknow!

It was, however, the fact that the Lady Dufferin and Balrampore Hospitals adjoin the grounds of the Christian College that probably weighed most in favour of this site for the new Medical College. Nor were the College authorities left long in doubt as to the determination of the Government. A short time after the visit already referred to, word came to the Principal that His Honor the Lieutenant-Governor would be pleased to meet representatives of the Christian College on a certain morning at Hosainabad, for the purpose of pointing out what seemed to them an eligible site for the Christian College! And thus, thirty-five years after we had as a Mission left Hosainabad for a new home, we were led back by the Government to a site only half a mile from the place where our first school in Lucknow had risen and fallen. Well was it for our College that on that day when the Great British Government pointed to a new site (in itself a most magnificent one) to which they proposed now to move us, and pointed with a finger which had back of it less persuasion than power, well was it we could say that more than thirty years ago we had left this very locality in order to find a more central location, that to move back now would mean death to an institution whose every interest lay in the great centre where for thirty-five years all agencies of the Mission had been in operation to build up an allround, well developed work—religious, educational and publishing. Nevertheless Government held out liberal inducements for us to make the change, but the College authorities stood firmly on a statement the force of which even His Honor could not deny.

The first temptation having failed we were led two miles east into the very centre of our work. We had pleaded for a unified work we should have it! No open ground being available, the Government would clear a site for us! It was all but humorous then, and altogether so now. For more than an hour His Honour, followed by a train worthy of the tail of a resplendent comet, pointed out beautiful sites to men who neither could nor wished to see any beauty in them, men who, however, needed not to deny the beauty of any site in order to carry the day, for the Government now was overlooking important considerations when it asked us to vacate a portion of the city where we were the only educational institution and enter a section already over-supplied with two good High Schools. Three sites were pointed out, and then the search ended. His Honor seemed, however, not to be discouraged, and his parting words were that the College might have two weeks in which to determine upon a new site, for the old site could not be held.

Then the College and its many friends betook themselves to prayer. They recalled the words of the infant Church in the times of the apostles— "and now Lord behold their threatenings." It seemed difficult—imposible—to interpret God's providences through all this long course of years in such a way as to think that we must at last relinquish that God-given site. But if it came to the worst, it was better to propose a site to the Government than to have them propose one to us. Accordingly, a few days later the whole missionary force of our Church in Lucknow led by Bishop Warne, went out to examine a possible site discovered by one of our number. For several days every available site in the city had been looked up, and this seemed the best, such as it was. We were not, however, called upon to make a request for it. Had it ever been asked for, it is a question whether or not Government would have given it. For the interest of posterity the site may be described. It was the land which lies East of the tombs on Neill Road, running from the Kaiserbagh Road to Quinton Road, and extending back to Kaiserbagh, the Central Training School and Zahur Bakhsh. This section of land on the North-East includes the house and property of the great Raja of Jahangirabad. He saw our party and came out to enquire the meaning of the presence of so many gentlemen. On being told, and being assured that the matter had gone so far that we were praying earnestly over it, he clasped his hands and said, "Pray for me too, that I may not lose my land!" He feared that had we put in a request for the land, the Government might have granted it!

The College did not make the mistake of putting up a fight and defying Government. It merely pointed out the tremendous difficulties involved, both to itself and the cause of education in the city, in moving from its present site. A letter of this tone was sent to His Honour stating that no suitable site could be found, indicating educational difficulties involved, and respectfully requesting a reconsideration of the matter. This letter is dated November 22, 1905. There is reason to believe, however, that even before it was received the Government had decided themselves to take the site at Shah Mina first proposed to us. However that may be, a prompt reply from Government House was received by Mr. Bare which is signed by His Honour's Private Secretary and reads as follows:—

"In reply to your letter dated the 22nd instant, I am desired to say that in view of the difficulty mentioned by you it has been decided to erect the Medical College on the

Shah Mina site; and there is now no idea of asking the Reid Christian College to give up their land."

Thus was settled in favour of the Christian College a momentous issue, and thus was passed a great crisis. The crisis once passed, there seems no possibility of our ever being called upon to face a similar problem. Whatever arguments there were on our side, and they were considerable, whatever influences may have worked in our behalf, there can be no doubt that His hand Who many years before had placed us in such a magnificent site, held us secure and in the hour of anxiety and danger was our support.

The year 1905 is for another reason full of significance for the College. That was the year which marked the beginning of the great Revival in India. The movement when towards the close of the year it reached our work in North India, in our schools took the form of a consecration of lives to the Ministry of the Church. In our own Lucknow School and College it ushered in an entirely new era, the significance of which the writer must pause to point out.

The greatness of the Revival in the Lucknow School and College will be realized when it is known that where in 1904 there but two young men who had signified their intention of entering the Ministry, there are to-day twenty-four of its choicest young men both in the College and High School who have consecrated their lives to this great work. When they complete their education, they will step out into the service of the Master. Should not this set all the bells in Methodism pealing! Those who know most of the previous spirit of hopelessness concerning our educated young men and their attitude towards Christian work will rejoice most now.

This work of the Revival is nothing short of epochal. A new day has dawned, for the tide of selfishness has been turned backwards. Within a year of the time the Revival first broke out in our schools in North India, more than a hundred young men had enthusiastically offered themselves for the Ministry of the Methodist Episcopal

Church—a year before there were not ten! These young men have entered a door of opportunity such as no young men of preceding ages ever had set before them. We rejoice that Satan was not able to close it. What tides of surging selfishness were there hurled back, what worldly ambitions were there overcome, none may ever know save he who suffered there a notable defeat and He who gave the glorious victory. A great reproach has been rolled away from that institution which, having experienced opposition even in its fonding, has by many been thought to be doing very little real missionary work through all these years. And now our Christian College is understood at last—*an institution breathing at the very heart of our success in this land!* Not the most short-sighted can fail now to see the vast significance of her work. But blessed are those who believed without seeing; who in a time of narrow vision and small faith looked upwards and gained that broader view, that more triumphant faith, which enabled them to see from the beginning the greatness of the work which God could accomplish through a Christian College. The visions and voices of those few alike went largely unheeded, but God has in these last days seen fit to speak through the Revival, and once for all justify our educational work. To be leaders at once in both intellectual and spiritual work is, indeed, the attainment of the highest ideal. The long night of toiling is over. As the dawn streaks the eastern sky, the Master draws nigh and bids us "Launch out into the deep." We are launching out, and the scene of our many labours is to become the scene of His triumphant power.

No account of this great work connected with the Revival of 1905-6, which appeared in our institution at Lucknow and caused such a transformation there, could be considered complete which left out of account the part played by a young man, one of India's own sons. His name is already well-known in Christian circles all over north India—it is Jashwant Rao Chitambar. Reid Christian College claims him with pride as

THE REV. BISHOP J.M. THOBURN D.D.
THE REV. J.M. REID. D.D.
THE REV. J. H. MESSMORE.
THE REV. T. S. JOHNSON. M.D.
THE REV. BISHOP E.W. PARKER D.D.

the first young man to complete his course of studies leading to the degree of B. A., and then to step into the ministry of the Methodist Episcopal Church. Five years ago he fought the battle against selfishness and worldly ambition, by the help of God was victor, and set an example for which American Methodism owes him a lasting debt of gratitude. To honor him is the delight of the Church and the College. Sustained as he is by the grace of God, and equipped as he is for magnificent service, he has doubtless a great career before him as a servant of God in India. At the time of the Revival in 1905 he was Headmaster of our High School in Lucknow, and to his example and words was due in considerable measure the remarkable movement among our educated young men towards the ministry of the Church.

It may be remarked that the history of this College has been written without a single reference to the wives of the men to whom goes the credit of making the College what it is to-day. This is not, however, because the work has not felt the influence of woman's heart and hand. History does not show, and the world can never know what a noble part the womanhood of our missionary body played in this great educational work. So persistent and far-reaching has been their influence from the beginning until the present day, but at the same time so hard to define, that it would be folly for the writer of this history to attempt to reduce it to words. Only those whose hands have been strengthened, whose hearts have been comforted, whose disappointments and discouragements have been shared and lightened, who have found at home an unfailing inspiration when the burdens of the work bore heavily, and in the midst of perplexities or grave problems have turned to the unfailing spring of sympathy and advice at home—only they will know how much this College owes to that noble band of women who shared with their husbands the separation from native land and loved ones, without on the one hand enjoying any adequate recognition of the great amount of missionary work actually done by them, or on the other the advantage of being so occupied by public affairs as to often forget the inconveniences and heart-hunger consequent on living in a foreign land. The College delights in honoring these not unknown but unheralded heroes!

In concluding this history the writer is conscious that while those who have been directly connected with the affairs of the institution have been indicated and their share in the work referred to, there are many whose names do not here appear, who also should be counted among the makers of the Lucknow Christian College. Especially does this apply with reference to the Board of Trustees of the College, who from year to year have ungrudgingly given their service to further the interests of this enterprise. In recent years the Rev. J. W. Robinson, not only by virtue of his appointment as Presiding Elder of the Oudh District but also because of a genuine interest in this great educational work, has merited and enjoyed the sincere gratitude of the College. As a member of the Board of Trustees he has been of great assistance in the counsels of the institution, and as an advisor and friend has proved his devotion at all times. To him and to others the College returns the warmest thanks, and trusts that the flight of years will see no diminution of such loyal friends.

The historian has spent much time looking backward. In it all, nothing has seemed more striking to him than the very unfavourable circumstances under which the work was begun, and the phenomenal success which has attended it. A city which fifty or sixty years ago, as the capital of a Mohammedan kingdom, was closed to the preaching of the Gospel by its fanatical and bigoted race of Moslem rulers, aud where the very idea of educating the public was wanting, is to-day one of the chief religious and educational centres ln the Empire. The city of which in 1824 Bishop Heber said, "It would not be expedient at present to send a missionary here," and the spirit of which was described by the Rev. W. Greenwood, who was Residency Chaplain at Lucknow from 1832-36, as so violent and fanatical that he thought Christian preaching in public would be only at the risk of life, this city has to-day a larger missionary force in it than any other inland city of India! It is this city which boasts of seven* High Schools and two† Colleges for the sons of those very fanatics of fifty years ago, and a splendidly equipped Christian High School and College for their daughters.

This magnificent work the historian cannot characterize otherwise than as a work of Faith--Divine Faith. The work which in 1856 was considered by a Government official madness to attempt, the work which the gallant Sir James Outram who led the advance in the capture of the city and the relief of the *Residency* thought "ought not to be attempted in such a country as Oudh," that work has been accomplished, to the glory of God, with signal success.

It was work of faith in God—a faith which

---

* Of these three are Christian Schools.

† Including Reid Christian College.

first shone most clear in the dying Sir Henry Lawrence. "Let a Christian Mission be established in Lucknow," said that great man as his life ebbed from the wound of a rebel shot. That was the voice of not only a Christian soldier but of a Christian seer: the voice of one who did not stop to count profit and loss, did not consider how great the danger might be or how great the probability of failure, did not question the literalness of Christ's command to go into all the world and preach the Gospel to every creature, but in the darkest moment had the unfailing light of divine faith, made practical to the extent of making it applicable to *any* circumstances. That was faith, and within quarter of a mile of the place where rests the mortal body of that immortal Christian hero, rise heavenward the towers of our Christian College and Christian School proclaiming to all the world that the faith of Henry Lawrence has been justified. Standing to-day at the grave of him "who tried to do his duty", while the imagination goes back to those bloody days in which he ended his great career, and the mind is busy thinking of that great dying injunction, you may hear the joyful peal of school bells summoning to Christian halls of learning: and from the tower of the famous *Residency*, where the great man sealed his loyalty to his God and his sovereign with his own blood, may be seen the spires of many Christian Churches pointing Godward the passer-by.

APPENDIX.

CHAPTER I.

The Need of Christian Education in India.

The need is as vast as the Indian Empire, as great as the ignorance and superstition of wellnigh three hundred million people can make it. There are few fields in the world for the Christian educator, such as is India in this twentieth century.

Much has been said and much written on this subject, but so long as opposition, open or concealed, both on the foreign field and in the home lands, finds a voice and wields influence, so long will there be the necessity of presenting the truth concerning this important matter. In advancing a few thoughts in this connection the writer would like to point out, first, the actual need of education in India and the burden of responsibility which rests upon every true philanthropist to help supply it, and next to show

" My people are destroyed for lack of knowledge."

INDIA'S IGNORANCE!

219 millions illiterate; 13 millions literate.

Each square represents one million.

(Figures for British India.)

that the Christian College is best fitted to give the education which India needs.

1. The actual need of education.

The reign of ignorance in India is not yet ended. To those who are not acquainted with the vastness of her territory and population, the educational statistics of this country will come as a surprise and a revelation. There are many who probably have bright visions of what *must*, as they suppose, have resulted after the expenditure of two hundred years of Protestant energy upon this land, and after some of the best missionary blood of Europe and America has for nearly two centuries mingled with the forces that are at work in the heart of this great empire.

The most effective way of letting in the light on this part of the question is to quote the latest educational statistics compiled by the Government of India. The figures are for British India only, including a total population of nearly two hundred and thirty-two million people. The following table taken from the census of 1901, shows the proportion of illiteracy in each of the great political divisions :—

British India	Totally Illiterate.	Literate.
Bengal	70,550,531	4,194,335
United Provinces of Agra and Oudh ...	46,212,917	1,478,865
Madras	35,803,347	2,406,089
Punjab and N.-W. Frontier	21,598,716	857,103
Bombay	17,383,545	1,176,016
Central Provinces ...	9,582,098	294,548
Assam	5,903,957	222,386
Burma	8,139,651	2,223,962
Berar	2,630,700	132,316
Ajmere	444,824	32,088
Coorg	166,540	14,067
	218,416,826	13,022,775

Such is the dense ignorance of India whose suave *Swamis*, visiting and lecturing in England and America, so often succeed in proving to their Western auditors is a country of great enlightenment—sufficiently great to even send representatives to the civilized countries of the occident and give those lands an opportunity of learning from the orient ! Yes, this is the boasted enlightenment of India even after the great British Government has for many decades brought her energies to bear upon the stupendous undertaking of educating her masses.

The Need of Christian Education.

Lest the awful significance of the figures above quoted should escape the casual reader, a special diagram has been prepared which condenses the statistics in such a way as to appeal directly to the eye. The diagram will give some adequate idea of the appalling need in India of education—even of the most primary kind, without which the social condition of any country is a hopeless one, allowing of no progress in any line. The accompanying diagram most surely indicates a country groaning under the hopeless tyranny of ignorance—nay, the case is not so hopeful even as that, for to "groan" implies the recognition of an evil, while the great masses of these people do not know enough to know that they need the light! Let the reader look at the diagram and then think! Think of two hundred and nineteen million people, best described as those of Nineveh—"persons that cannot discern between their right hand and their left hand"! Truly says the word of God—"*My people are destroyed for lack of knowledge.*" Cannot these words take on new meaning for us?

Appendix.

Along with a general view, such as we have now taken of British India as a whole, it may be interesting for a while to confine our attention to a limited area of this great Indian Empire. To members of the Methodist Episcopal Church, no field of mission work is of more interest than what has been called " The Heart of India." This section includes Oudh which is often referred to as " The Garden-spot of India"—one of the most thickly populated and best known sections of this land. On the map it is marked " The United Provinces of Agra and Oudh"; or (if the map be more than five years old) it will be found designated " The North-West Provinces."

The special interest which attaches to the United Provinces is, that it is the scene of the earliest labours of our Church in this land—the place where the Methodist Episcopal Church worked out its educational problems. It is, therefore, not only associated with the beginning of our great missionary enterprise, but is the home of our colleges and oldest institutions. This is the

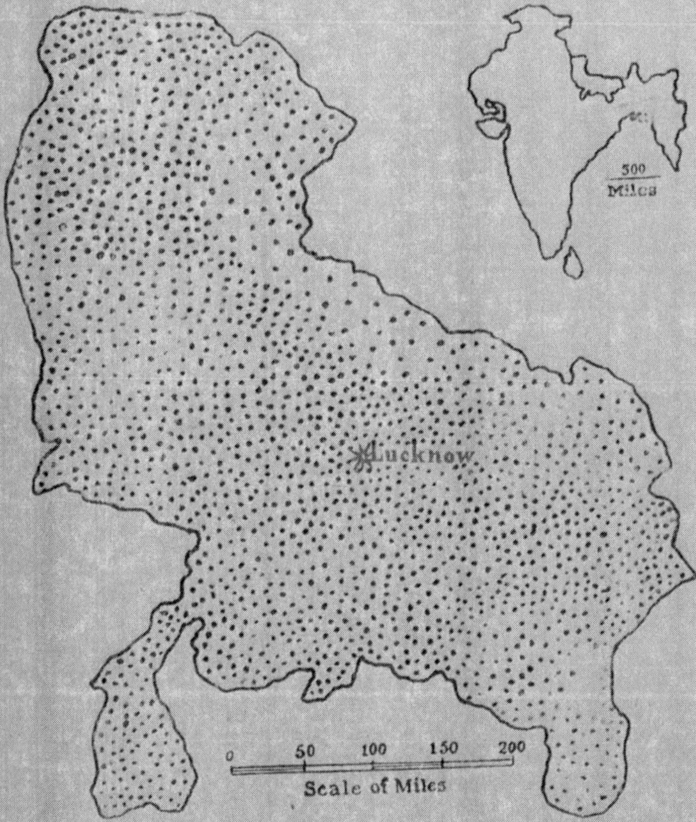

THE UNITED PROVINCES OF AGRA AND OUDH.

Each black dot represents 25,674 illiterate persons.

Total illiterate .. 46,212,917

Total literate ... 1,478,865

field where Dr. William Butler laid the foundation of our work, and this the scene of the early years of Bishop Thoburn's great career. Here Miss Thoburn poured forth the perfume of her holy life, and here the sainted Phoebe Rowe lived and died. That tremendous worker of our Church, Bishop E. W. Parker, found here a field which gave full scope for all his powers, and during the forty years of his missionary life he never worked anywhere else. Here our Evangelist-Bishop Warne, has done his best work in India, and sees nothing but fields white unto the harvest all around him. Here also have toiled those giants of the early days whose record is written only in heaven. Here for fifty years our beloved Church has laboured and prayed, and we may turn to it now with special interest.

The United Provinces of Agra and Oudh contain somewhat over forty-seven million people, a population nearly equal to that of the German Empire. When we look at this field from the educational point of view we are oppressed with what confronts

The reign of ignorance is supreme. What an astounding fact it is that out of a total population of 47,691,782, only 1,478,865 are able to read and write their own names! These are the latest Government statistics, and they show that the United Provinces return the greatest percentage of illiteracy among the great divisions of British India.

The accompanying outline map of the United Provinccs of Agra and Oudh aims to indicate more clearly how astonishing is the percentage of illiteracy in this great Province. It will serve also to show what a strategic centre is its chief city, Lucknow, the home of our Christian College. No large city of the Provinces is more centrally situated than is Lucknow, and none affords a more magnificent field for the full operations of a Christian College. Surely here is a great need of the educator, if the densest and most wide-spread ignorance ever constituted a need.

II.—*Let us turn now to note what part the Christian College plays and should play in supplying this great need.*

The Need of Christian Education.

There is no more vital work in any great mission field than the education of the people. There never can be either progress or self-support without it. It is not without good reason that the great Missionary Societies represented in India have given much of their money, many of their best men and a great part of their best thought to the up-building of their educational institutions. Professor Borden P. Bowne, during his recent visit to India, said to the writer: "If you had to give up either the educational or the purely evangelistic work, you would do wisely to continue the educational agencies." If this holds true, it is, of course, because *Christian* education is what our mission schools impart.

The work of education, however, even apart from the direct Christian influences which are brought to bear upon the student while in school, is itself of vast importance. To put a man into the way of reading the Bible for himself, is to make him responsible for his choice so soon as the Bible is in his hands. The question of sending the *preacher* is solved when God's own message can be thus had direct.

Considering the question from another point of view, we are equally convinced that even secular education has a great part to play in the redemption of India from darkness and superstition. It has been well said that "Caste is the keystone to the arch of Hinduism." Note that this really presents a social rather than a religious problem. What a Hindu *believes* is not of foremost importance. If he conforms to the rules of caste, he is really free to believe what he wishes. Education, then, is of supreme importance if it helps to undermine the system of caste. And this is exactly what it is doing; especially in our mission schools does it serve to obliterate caste distinctions, and the process of undermining this great Hindu stronghold is going on in our own sight. Let us not talk of wasting time "merely teaching school." Let us look through to the end and see the mighty results, hidden only to eyes that will not see.

Someone says—It is the work of the British Government to cope with this educational problem. No one will deny this, but it is likewise true that it is our duty to help in a work which is too great for any Government. Remember, also, that the hands of England are tied in regard to the most important element of education—the moral and religious. The kind of education Government imparts is good, but it is not good enough ; it does not meet India's great need. The moral and spiritual side of the student in a Government institution is absolutely untouched. This is the result of circumstances which the great majority of English officials regret and deplore, but which they cannot see their way to overcome. It lies, therefore, with our missionary educational institutions to reach the heart and soul life of India's students. We teach the Bible openly and fearlessly, and our halls are crowded.

Government is not indifferent or inactive in regard to the great problem of India's *moral* education. An Education Commission, appointed more than twenty years ago, raised the question of moral education in the schools and colleges of India. Even then were only too apparent the evils of the policy of neutrality on the part of Government in all matters pertaining to the religion and morality of the people. In the schools the result of this policy was long ago seen to be most deplorable. From time to time Government and government officials have made distinct utterances on this subject, showing not only a desire to deal with this most important matter, but indicating that the best solution lay in "aided schools and Colleges in which religious instruction is prominently recognized." Here then is the opportunity of the Christian College.

Educational conditions in the Philippine Islands afford a striking contrast to those in India. In those Islands, out of a total child population of school-going age amounting to 1,200,000, there are 300,000 already enrolled in the public schools. That is to say, one out of every four is already provided for, and in one generation the whole country will be not only literate but

English-speaking. Who can doubt the great factor this will prove itself in the ultimate regeneration of those Islands? In British India, the proportion of literate to illiterate is only one to eighteen, or $5\frac{1}{2}$ per cent., and her day of redemption from the densest ignorance seems very far removed. How sadly India suffers in a comparison with Japan also! In that progressive Eastern country, the number of those who are literate is actually 90 per cent. This is little short of wonderful, and is the fruit of such an educational awakening as India has not yet thought possible, but of which her need is appalling!

When we limit our field of vision so as to look at the educational problem as related only to the womanhood of India, we are confronted by facts even more startling. There are in British India fourteen million girls of school-going age, and out of this immense number only 405,000 are under any instruction. Only one girl out of every thirty-four receiving even a primary education! And the rest?—growing up to motherhood without even a word of learning or an iota of sympathy for anything of the kind. Let American mothers think of their own daughters in such a condition, and then face the problem anew. Think, by way of contrast, of Japan having 98 per cent. of her girls of school-going age under instruction, with a total number of 60,000 public schools for the education of her youth!

Among the girls of India, education lies almost wholly in the hands of lady missionaries. A Government Inspectress of Schools recently said to a missionary's wife: "Why don't you missionaries give up the teaching of Christianity in your schools? If you would only do so, you would have female education in India entirely in your hands." This implies that Government is utterly unable to cope with the problem aside from the co-operation of lady missionaries. Should the work of the Missionary Societies cease, most of the work would come to an end. On whom lies the heavier burden—whose is the greater responsibility?

During this last year the Government has

undertaken anew to arouse public opinion on this great question of the education of India's womanhood, but what is for it a comparatively new field has been for forty years familiar ground for our own Church, and for a much longer period has been worked in by older Missionary Societies. Government can learn much from experienced missionary workers. How stupendous the work is may be realized when it is known that of the one hundred and forty million women of India, not even one million are able to read or write.

The key to the whole educational problem in India is in the hands of the Missionary Societies. If India's young manhood and womanhood are to be truly educated, and to be led out into lives of moral as well as intellectual grandeur, the work must be done by missionary agencies. Not only so, but it must be done soon. The tide is fast setting to selfishness, worldliness and scepticism. When another generation has passed, it will be far harder to turn it back. The great opportunity for Christianity in India may by that time have been irretrievably lost, and a hundred years of effort may then fail to accomplish what twenty could now do.

How terrible has been the grip of the powers of darkness! Is it to be supposed that this condition of affairs will rectify itself, and that a people who, after so many years of British rule and two hundred years of missionary effort, are still busy raising barriers to progress, will of themselves bring order out of chaos and light into darkness? Add to the natural obstacles those which are raised by religion, and it will be seen how vain is it to expect the Indians to make any great movement, for the present anyway, towards the imparting of even a primary education to those who sit in darkness.

Religious prejudice is a positive force making against enlightenment in India. Hinduism turns to the institutes of her great legendary lawgiver, Manu, and reads from pages soiled by forty centuries of handling, words which make it impossible to strike a single blow at the intellectual shackles that bind the lower class. Mahommedanism turns with a shrug of the shoulders to Fate, and says—*When such seems Allah's will, why seek to overturn it?* Or it points with pride to the *Koran* and says—*Here is the storehouse of universal knowledge; let those who seek light take freely from it.* It was in this spirit that the Khalipha Omar is said to have remarked, when the fate of the great Alexandrian library was at stake—"If the books are contrary to the *Koran* they are blasphemous; if they are beyond it they are superfluous: let them burn."

The influence of the educated class in India is tremendous; perhaps in no country is it greater. Not only does education put power into the hands of those who obtain knowledge, but to begin with, the great majority of Indian students are of the upper and most influential class. Thus it is doubly important to reach them. It is not their number which is of the greatest consequence. In all the Colleges and in the two upper classes of the High Schools of this land, there are probably fewer than 125,000 students, and in all India there are, it may be estimated, under three and a half million English-speaking natives of the country. These men, however, hold virtually all the power—political and social—which is entrusted to-day to India's hands by the British Government and the sanctions of society. *Such men must be reached by the truth!* If the Cross of Christ does not sway them, the Trident of Hinduism and the Crescent of the Moslem will wield, to their eternal los the destinies of one-fifth of the inhabitants of this globe! The imparting of mere secular education will not meet the necessities of the case. India will arise some day and adjust herself to the conditions of the modern era, but her religious ideals will remain what they are, unless the Church of Christ arouse herself to meet the great emergency and the unparalleled opportunity.

Every argument in favour of Christian Colleges and Universities in nominally Christian lands applies with additional force to such institutions in non-Christian countries. If society, as a whole, be looked at, then pagan communities, bound by the shackles of heathenism, should stir us to redoubled efforts; if on the other hand, the Church itself be regarded, then the infant Church, struggling amidst unparalleled darkness, against tremendous odds, to preserve life and render growth possible, deserves and must have all the help which Christian education can give.

If it is our duty to "educate Christianity and Christianize education," then the Christian College is indispensable; if it is true that "Christianity must educate itself if it is to perpetuate itself," then again the Christian College stands on an immovable rock. Regarded from any aspect whatever, the Christian College is an indispensable adjunct to the Church, a necessary part of the Kingdom of Christ.

A great educator in America says:—"What is most needed in the educational world is an ethical revival at the very heart of education;" and one of the greatest educationists in India said many years ago—"If India is to be regenerated—if her rising generation is destined to make any progress—it must be achieved by a sound system of education and by a wide diffusion of morality." This work, in India as elsewhere, the Christian College stands ready to do.

CHAPTER II.

What the Christian College Teaches.

The Christian College in India, like every other College, is affiliated to one or another of the five great Universities of the land. The curricula are, therefore, determined in each case by the University in question. In this respect the Christian College does not differ from any other College. The system of education which prevails does not allow of any choice as to subjects or courses of study; these are all prescribed and even the text-books are either indicated or suggested.

There is, however, an important respect in which the teaching of the Christian College differs from that of all other institutions of education. This is in the imparting of distinctly religious teaching, which is done systematically, the Bible being taken up as a regular text-book and instruction being given every day. In our Christian College at Lucknow, and elsewhere also, attendance in the scripture class is compulsory, the student being given to understand this on his application for admission. Along with this the Chapel service, with which the work of the day is always begun, does its share in conveying religious and moral truth to the hearts of all. This opening exercise consists of a Christian hymn, the reading of a Psalm responsively, and of the Lord's Prayer. In these public devotions all are invited to participate, the attendance itself being required.

This amount of religious instruction which in our Christian College occupies half an hour each day, is in the case of Christian students supplemented, of course, by the regular teaching of the Church, the Sunday School, the Young Men's Christian Association and other similar organizations.

The value of the religious instruction thus given in the Christian Colleges of India has never been rightly appreciated by those who not only have felt but have boldly said that higher education had either no place or a very insignificant place in Christian

Missionary work. The extent of the good thus accomplished may not be evident yet, but in the present period of transition in India there is no factor which is more essential than the educational one. When the process of the disintegration of pagan faiths, which is now visible on every hand, has been brought to a completion and heathen India has felt to its heart the thrill of Christian life, the historian of those great days—which may be nearer than most of us suppose—will set down the Christian educational institutions of the past as foremost among the agents which brought about the transformation and regeneration of a nation.

The great Dr. Duff, the father of missionary educational institutions in India, argued that the work of such institutions was most effective in preparing for the overthrow of the false religion of Hinduism, by undermining the whole cosmogony to which she is inseparably wedded. In this work Science and Philosophy, History and English Literature play a part more important even than that played by direct religious teaching.

Whether, therefore, the Christian College be regarded as an agency for the development of the Church itself, or be looked at as an instrument in the hands of the Church for the tearing down of heathen strongholds, it will be seen to be doing not only an indispensable work but a work which no other institution can perform.

With these facts before us, it will be of interest to take a glance at the courses of study which find a place in the Christian Colleges of India. To many the wide range of subjects as well as the advanced nature of the studies will be a surprise. It must, of course, be borne in mind that since in the case of languages a selection is always open to the student, only those are taught in which courses may be desired. In an oriental country Sanskrit, Arabic and Persian are naturally most often chosen.

The affiliation of our Christian College at Lucknow being to the Allahabad University the prospectus subjoined is that which obtains in Colleges affiliated to this University. As regards the other Universities of India it differs, however, only in minor matters. At the end of the second year of College work the student is required to appear for an examination which is termed the Intermediate Examination. The course of studies prescribed for this examination is as follows:—

I. English.—Tennyson, *The Passing of Arthur;* Matthew Arnold, *Sohrab and Rustum*; Beesly, *Elizabeth*; Froude, *English Seamen in the 16th Century*, or Blackie's *Self-culture.*

II. Classical Languages.—Sanskrit, Arabic, Persian (with Arabic), Latin, Greek, Hebrew.

III. Modern Language.—French.

IV. History.—Either English History, *viz.*, *A Student's History of England* by Gardiner, or

Ancient History, *viz.*, Merivale and Puller, *School History of Rome* and C. A. Fyffe, *Greece.*

V. Deductive Logic—(Syllabus prescribed.)

VI. Mathematics—Algebra, Trigonometry, Geometry of Conic Sections, Geometry of solids, Co-ordinate Geometry.

VII.—Physics—Heat, Light, Sound, Magnetism, Electricity and Mechanics.

VIII. Chemistry—Inorganic (Syllabus prescribed).

The text-books prescribed in the above courses are those which will be required in 1908. The books may be varied from time to time, though the amount of work required does not change.

When the student has successfully completed his course of studies, and has passed the examination set not by his College but the University, he may continue his studies for the degree of Bachelor of Arts. In choosing his subjects from the course required for the Intermediate Examination, the student must be guided by the following regulation: The studies are grouped so as to form two courses, of which the student may select either. The "A" Course is comprized of:—English, a Classical Language, History and Deductive,

Logic or Mathematics. The "B" Course consists of:—English, Mathematics, Physics and Chemistry.

When the student has passed the Intermediate Examination of the University, he may proceed to the studies leading up to the B.A. degree, to complete which requires two years more. The studies for this course must be selected, according to University regulations, from the following :—

I. ENGLISH—Shakespeare, *Macbeth*, *A Midsummer Nights Dream;* Milton, *L'Allegro Il Penseroso*, *Lycidas;* Tennyson, *Selections* (by Rowe and Webb); George Eliot, *Silas Marner;* Sidney Lee, *Shakespeare's Life and Work;* Hamerton, *The Intellectual Life;* Dowden, *Shakespeare Primer;* Gwynn's *Masters of English Literature.*

II. CLASSICAL LANGUAGES—Latin, Greek, Hebrew, Arabic, Arabic-Persian, Sanskrit.

III. MATHEMATICS.—Algebra, Trigonometry, Analytical Geometry, Differential Calculus, Integral Calculus, Dynamics, Hydrostatics.

IV. PHILOSOPHY—Mill,—*Utilitarianism*; Muirhead, *Ethics*; Jame's, *Psycohlogy*; Fraser, *Selections from Berkeley;* Flint, *Theism* or Sidgwick, *Outlines of the History of Ethics*.

V. POLITICAL ECONOMY—Walker, *Political Economy*; A. Marshall, *Principles of Economics*; H. de B. Gibbin's *Industrial History of England;* J. N. Keyne's *Scope and Method of Political Economy.*

VI. HISTORY—*(a)* Modern European History:—Freeman, *General Sketch of European History Michelet*, *Precis de l' Histoire* Moderne (Translated); C. W. Oman, *England in the 19th Century;* Alison Phillips, *Modern Europe, from 1815, and* (*b*) Indian History:—Vincent Smith, *The Early History of India;* Lane-Poole, *Medieval India;* Lyall, *Rise of the British Dominion in India;* Strachey, *India.* or (c) Medieval European History:—Freeman *General Sketch of European History;* Thatcher and Schevill, *Europe in the Middle Ages;* Robinson, *History of Western Europe;* Freeman, *Essays on Frederick Barbarossa and Fredrick II.*

What the Christian College Teaches.

The regulation which governs a student's choice of studies from the above course is as follows —

"Every candidate for the B.A. degree shall be required to show a competent knowledge of three distinct branches of study. The branches recognized are —

Group A.—English.

Group B.—Classical Language and Mathematics.

Goup C.—Philosophy, Political Economy, History. It shall be open to the candidate to offer himself for examination in English and any two subjects in Group B. or in (1) English, (2) any one subject in Group B. and (3) any one subject in Group C."

In addition to these courses, the University offers courses leading to the following degrees :—Master of Arts, Bachelor of Science, Master of Science, Doctor of Science, Bachelor of Laws and Master of Laws. As these courses are not offered by our Christian College in Lucknow, the details and text books will not be given. It is hoped, however, that at no distant date our College can open a class for those desirous of getting the degree of Bachelor of Science. In due course of time our Christian College will probably be able to provide also for the course of studies leading to the degree of Master of Arts.

CHAPTER III.

The Outlook.

The outlook of the Christian College in India at the beginning of the 20th century is most inspiring. There never was a time when its work in this land was more highly valued or better understood. Its detractors have been many, but their mouths have been effectually shut as the great work of the Christian College has become apparent and its great purposes have unfolded themselves.

It will be interesting and the same time conducive to the strengthening of faith to regard this great object for a while through the eyes of eminent Englishmen who in years past occupied high positions in the Government of India and who have spoken out of a large experience. Their words uttered during the last decade of the century which has just closed, are true of the Christian College to-day, and when we rightly appreciate what these institutions have done and are doing, we shall better understand why the outlook is so bright. A few short extracts are given below :—

"I have no hesitation whatever in saying that it would be a calamity for India if missionary schools were withdrawn. Apart from immediate conversion to the faith, their influence on the mind of the people has been of *inestimable* value."—SIR WILLIAM MUIR, K.C.S.I., D.C.L., LL.D., Ex-Principal of the University of Edinburgh, formerly Secretary to the Government of India, Lieutenant-Governor of the North-West Provinces, etc.

"Personally I am convinced that any system of conversion which excluded the general and indirect work of preparation done by the mission schools and colleges, would distinctly lower the status of Christianity in India."—SIR WILLIAM WILSON HUNTER, K.C.S.I., M.A., (Oxon), LLD.

"So far from drawing back, it is more than ever the duty of the Church to go forward in its educational policy. God forbid that I should undervalue preaching and evangelizing. I believe India is only waiting for some native St. Paul to turn by thousands to the Lord. But the more active you are in your schools the better you will be prepared for that day when it comes Even now, as a matter of fact, although statistics of conversion are not a true test of the value of missionary work, the most numerous converts and the best are made in the schools."—SIR CHARLES U. AITCHISON, K.C.S.I., C.I.E., LL.D., formerly Lieutenant-Governor of the Punjab.

"In so far as the existing educational system leads men to reject Hinduism, it prepares the way for Christianity. But if no effort is made to teach Christianity and if Christian schools and colleges were closed, atheism would be unchecked until some extension of Brahmoism or some new sect like the Brahmos arose."—SIR CHARLES E. BERNARD, K.C.S.I., formerly Home Secretary of the Indian Government and Chief Commissioner of Burma.

"There can be no doubt as regards the value and necessity of education in connection with Missions. Although the result of mission work may not be important, if tested by the number of conversions, the effect of Christian instruction imparted by mission schools has been very marked. The truths of Christianity and salvation through Jesus Christ alone have been made known widely; faith in Hinduism has been shaken, and the superstitions connected with it are only maintained through the influence of old Pundits and leading men who have had no school education."—THE HON. SIR HENRY RAMSAY, C.B., K.C.S.I.

"I feel assured of this fact, that educational missions have, under God's blessing, conferred a boon upon India, and have been permitted by Him to be the means of bringing many souls to Christ. I have long entertained a belief that His word is working secretly to an extent which we cannot perceive, and that the day is not far off when the number of those who are added to the Church will be as unexpected as was the draught of fishes after our Lord's resurrection. May we be prepared to meet it

I hope and pray the decision may not be that of abandoning educational missions, but of strengthening them and concentrating them."—SIR GEORGE EDWARD KNOX, Judge, United Provinces, High Court.

"The higher education has its effects good and bad, but mostly good, and it has an influence toward a better morality and a better religion enormously greater than any missionary statistics indicate. It will be a grave loss to the best interests of the Indian empire if the churches should abandon that part of the teaching of the Indian youth which they alone can give. Few, if any, of the attentive students of a missionary college leaves it without religious impression. In some of course, it is superficial, but in others it is deep. And it must not be supposed that it is not deep because it does not lead to public acceptance of the Christian creed. The time will come, I have long believed when there will be—quite suddenly—an adoption of the Christian faith so wide-spread as to be almost universal—probably not in my life-time.

The preparation for it demands the patient continuance of prolonged labour, but it will come when the times are ready and the man appears who has the qualification for an apostolate. In this preparation the missionary colleges are playing the principal part, a part much more real and penetrating, according to my means of judging, than that of even the missionary preacher." —SIR JOHN WOODBURN, Late Lieut.-Governor of Bengal.

Mr. John R. Mott, a few years ago said: "More and more India will be governed and its thought-life moulded by the student class. The burning question is, shall this leadership be heathen, agnostic or Christian? Universites and Colleges in their relation to the progress of Christianity are strategic points in the world's conquest. .... The work of Educational Missions in India is of transcendent importance. .... Educational missions have opened a larger number of doors for the preaching of the Gospel than any other agency. ...... They have furnished the most distinguished and influential converts and have done more than all else combined to undermine heathen superstitions and false systems of belief. . . . The field is not only vast and open, but ripe."

Surely the Lord who called Christian Colleges into existence in India, has given His servants the joy of seeing much accomplished through these great agencies. As for the future, the horizon ever widens as the work progresses.

Let us turn now to look for a while at the prospects that lie before the Christian College at Lucknow. We have traced its steady growth during the thirty years that have passed since the infant "Centennial" School saw the light, what will the next thirty years reveal?

As the year 1906 draws to a close all connected with our Christian College at Lucknow feel that the immediate future holds for it greater and better days than the institution has ever yet known. A glance at the various departments of its activity will give the reasons for such an expectation.

During 1906 two gifts, aggregating $23,000 have been realized by the College. This money, $15,000 of which came from the estate of Mrs. Coxe and $8,000 from that of Mrs. J. M. Reid, has provided for the erection of two most important buildings. Mrs. Coxe's money, as requested by her, is to go towards the erection of a fine hostel for our Christian students. The $15,000, which amounts to over Rs. 45,000, here in India, have been supplement by Rs. 25,000 the grant-in-aid from the Local Government. This handsome building grant from the Government both puts the seal of their approval on our work and makes it possible for us to plan for a Rs. 70,000 structure. The money will be wisely spent and will make possible such boarding accommodations for our ever-increasing number of Christian students as we have needed and desired for years. A handsome two-storey structure will be put up which when complete will probably be the finest boarding house owned by any Christian educational institution in the Provinces.

A portion of the money from Mrs. Reid's estate has been put into a much-needed residence for a College Professor. The house which is already well under way, is located next to the Boarding House with a view to its being occupied by a man who can give a good share of his time to the direct, personal management of the affairs of the Hostel. Such an arrangement is an ideal towards which the College has long been working. Its consummation will make it possible for the institution to exercise the strictest supervision of the morals of all the young men and boys who are entrusted to the care of the school. With such provisions for this very important part of the life of the institution, we can affirm with greater confidence than ever before that parents may feel safe in entrusting their sons to our care.

The remainder of Mrs. Reid's money will probably go towards the erection of a greatly needed Science Hall. This is a building which our College must have, as it is already looking towards an affiliation to the B.Sc. grade. The growth of any modern educational institution is impossible in these days without ample provisions being made for the scientific branch of education. India is itself undergoing a scientific *renaissance* and our College *must* measure up to the demands of the times. Where the money is to come from to provide for our Science Hall we do not know. A sum of at least $30,000 will be required for the building and its equipment. The Principal of the College and the Board of Trustees are doing their utmost to provide for this pressing emergency. It must be met, we know not how but feel sure that God who has in His Providence brought us to face the need will show us how to provide for it. Our Christian College still needs friends.

The outlook of the Lucknow Christian College will never be all that it should until some further demands have been met. Among the additional things upon which the greatest power and usefulness of this institution largely depend three may here be mentioned. *In the first place more Christian teachers and Professors are needed.* The educational need of India must not only be met soon, but it must be met by educational institutions worthy of the name. Our Missionary Schools and Colleges should be better equipped and manned than any others. Money must be spent without stint in order to provide the best of everything, and above all, the number of Christian teachers ought to be increased. So long as heathen teachers are, to any large extent, employed in our schools, our influence will be minimized and our work irremediably crippled. And yet the great majority of all our under-teachers, not only in Lucknow but elsewhere' are at present heathen. This is the case partly because Christian teachers are few and hard to get, and partly because non-Christian teachers usually work on lower salaries. The scarcity of Christian teachers will disappear of itself as our work progresses, but the financial standing of our schools must be bettered if we are to be enabled to do what common sense dictates as absolutely essential. Too much emphasis cannot be laid upon the employment of Christian teachers. Think of what a certain American educator said when asked by the Regents of one of the State Universities in America to accept the presidency; "Gentlemen, I understand that in the teaching force of the institution at the present time are three or four men who are openly and avowedly and aggressively antagonistic to the Christian faith. My acceptance of your offer must be conditioned upon the dismissal of these men from the teaching force. Do you now clean house at the beginning, and I will make it my business to see that the house is kept clean." That Board of Regents proceeded to remove the teachers who were antagonistic to Christianity, but most of our schools on this mission field are compelled—largely for lack of funds—to retain on their Staff, year after year, men who are fundamentally' both by nature and education, opposed to the cardinal principles of our belief. We, too, wish to "clean house" but we need help. Let

Christian people furnish us the means necessary to put carefully trained Christian teachers in the place of non-Christian, and we will see to it that our schools are kept clean of heathen influences. In the Lucknow College especially we need at least three endowed Professorships for Indian Christian men. But it takes $15,000 to endow such a Professorship and the question which the College repeats constantly is, *Where are the friends and philanthropists to be found who will endow these chairs?*

Among the many other needs which cannot be supplied without money, there is, secondly, that of a Normal School for the training of our Indian Christian teachers. Government has in the past five years entered upon a new era in regard to the training of teachers for its schools. A new type of teacher, bearing a Government certificate of normal training, is fast supplanting the old, self-made man. Another five years of such progress, and a great host of our Christian teachers must be admittedly antiquated. The emergency demands an efficient Normal

School for Christians—having a thoroughly Christian atmosphere, and giving training equal if not superior to that which is imparted in Government schools of a similar kind. We should not for a moment think of sending our Christian teachers to a godless Government Normal School. Their intellectual need would, doubtless, be met, but the influence there brought to bear on them would unfit them for the very work we require of them. Christian teachers who have lost touch with their Saviour—who have not a spiritual tone—are scarcely preferable to non-Christians. A wordly ideal such as Government schools impart is diametrically opposed to what we need. A thoroughly equipqed Normal Department added to the College would meet the need. This could become the trainnig school for Christian teachers not only of our own church, but for those of other Missions who might desire to avail themselves of such advantages under Christian influences.

The third of the great needs on which the success of the College was said to depend is a Boarding House for non-Christians. This need, while it is pressing in the extreme, can fortunately be more easily met than either that of Christian teachers or that of a Normal School, because the money required is not so much. Since this is a matter in which the Government always stands ready to help, we can safely count on their giving a sum equal to the amount which the College can raise for the purpose. If therefore we estimate that Rs. 30,000 will put up just such a building as in required, we need apply to the friends of the institution for only the small sum of Rs. 5,000. Here is a rare opportunity for an investor to double his money and provide for a most essential side of the life and activities of this great institution.

The need for a Boarding House for non-Christians may be stated thus:—Without such a building we can never hope to draw any considerable number of Hindu or Mohammedan students. Now our desire to greatly increase the number of our non-Christian students, aside from the general intention to elevate by educating, is made up chiefly of two elements. The first is that unless we can get access to these students we cannot hope to influence them for Christ. Anything, therefore, which will increase our non-Christian student-body will be helping the College to carry out its ideal as an evangelizing agency. In the next place, since non-Christian students almost invariably mean an increased income for the College through fees and tuition, we need them to help defray the expenses of the institution. These are the chief reasons for urging the claims of a Boarding House for non-Christians.

What is the outlook? It is all fair and beautiful, but these things must be attended to ere the Christian College at Lucknow can be what those heroic men intended who lived and died for it, or what it should be in the highest iterest of Christ's extending kingdom in this land.

THE END.